Stage Directing

Stage Directing

The First Experiences

Jim Patterson

University of South Carolina

WAVELAND

PRESS, INC.

Long Grove, Illinois

For information about this book, contact:
  Waveland Press, Inc.
  4180 IL Route 83, Suite 101
  Long Grove, Illinois 60047-9580
  (847) 634-0081
  info@waveland.com
  www.waveland.com

CONTENTS

2008 PREFACE

Stage Directing: The First Experiences introduces students to the basic steps in stage directing by leading them through the essential concepts a beginning stage director must know. It is a complete text on the basic principles of stage directing. However, it is not an encyclopedic reference text embodying everything every director should know. The book's conciseness offers teachers a chance to use this text together with their own additions—of exercises or subject matter—to create a meaningful, single-semester introduction to stage directing.

■ OVERVIEW

This book is organized around six logical steps that make up the directing process.

Step 1: Selecting the Playscript
Step 2: Analyzing and Researching the Playscript
Step 3: Conceiving the Production
Step 4: Casting: The Ideal and the Real
Step 5: Rehearsing: Staging, Shaping, Polishing
Step 6: Giving and Receiving Criticism

In addition to these six sections, the Prologue—The Director at Work—defines the role of the director and the Epilogue—Thinking Back and Looking Forward—provides review questions for contemplation and sets forth suggestions for the student's further growth as a director. Appendixes A and B contain two short plays that can be used as material for analysis and practical exercises. Appendix C, new to this printing, is a short history of the director in the modern and postmodern theatre.

Although this practical training manual is organized chronologically around the steps that the director must take to mount a production, it is my hope that teachers will find the format flexible. If Step 4: Casting is not appropriately placed for the course you are teaching, for example, it can easily be moved forward or included later in the course. If the "Sound Project" in Step 3 needs to be used elsewhere, it surely can be—and with my blessing! The same is true of Step 6: Giving and Receiving Criticism. Appendix C, The Director in the Modern and Postmodern Theatre: A Brief History, can be used as an introduction to directing, as a course conclusion, or anywhere else the instructor wishes to schedule it because it is a stand-alone essay. The teacher may also choose to omit this aspect of the book.

The exercises, called Experiences, are included so that the instructor can have choices; it was never my intent that every one be used or that they replace the ones the instructor favors. In short, I hope instructors will find this flexibility to their liking.

The exercises were created with the assumption that there will not be a design team, experienced or otherwise, to assist with the preparation of class projects. Instead, the beginning director will be responsible for creating the ground plan, gathering the furniture and hand props, collaborating with the actors to select from their personal wardrobes what they will wear in performance, and arranging the illumination.

▄▄▄ FEATURES

Stage Directing incorporates a number of features that I hope will engage both teachers and students, including the following:
- **Boxes.** Throughout the book the reader will discover boxes that contain practical directing tips.
- **Directing and the Web.** Links to pertinent Web sites will be found at the end of each directing step. Students can surf for further material by using the URLs cited.
- **Goals.** Each directing step will identify goals for the reader. These goals should alert the student to what is significant in each part of the book.
- **Key Terms.** Most of the directing steps conclude with a list of important terms. Students are urged to use these terms as a method for written review to determine their depth of understanding.
- **Examples.** The text illustrates many points with examples from modern and contemporary playscripts and productions. The examples are cast in such a way that the student need not have read the playscript or seen a particular production to understand the citation.
- **Experiences.** Each step and major section concludes with some basic exercises created to put directing precepts to a practical test.
- **Illustrations.** Over seventy charts, graphs, and photographs are included to visualize and exemplify the text. The captions also add substance to the ideas under discussion.

▄▄▄ PLAYS FOR DIRECTING EXPERIENCES

For the director's journey to be a manageable and practical one, the instructor is urged to consider very short one-act plays for the experiences devoted to the analysis of drama as well as for practical directing projects. Scenes from full-length playscripts or even substantial one-act scripts require the beginning director to spend hours cutting the text, a special skill in and of itself. Longer plays also tend to have larger casts and so can prove troublesome to cast and rehearse for classroom presentation.

    The following anthologies come from several 10-minute play collections, particularly those sponsored by the Actors Theater of Louisville. These collections of brief scripts will offer the beginning director the challenge of analyzing and shaping the entire arc of a play with actors in rehearsal. Because these plays are short, the casts are small—usually two to three actors—and there are limited scenic requirements. Incidentally, I have found that many of the plays actually run less than 10 minutes.

- *Instant Applause, Volume One: Twenty-six Very Short Complete Plays,* Blizzard Publishing, 1994.
- *Instant Applause, Volume Two: 30 Very Short Complete Plays*, Blizzard Publishing, 1998.
- *Take Ten: New 10-Minute Plays*, Vintage Books, 1997.
- *Ten-Minute Plays: Volume 3,* Samuel French, Inc., 1995.
- *Ten-Minute Plays: Volume 4*, Samuel French, Inc., 1998.
- *25 10-Minute Plays From Actors Theatre of Louisville*, Samuel French, Inc., 1989.

These anthologies may already be a part of your library's collection. If not, ask that they be ordered and put on limited reserve for your class. Add other 10-minute plays to your reserve list as they become available.

ACKNOWLEDGMENTS

I am deeply indebted to Kenneth Cameron, Sara Nalley, Elbin Cleveland, Donna McKenna-Crook, Joe Baldino, R. Scott Williams, and especially Philip Hill for their dedicated and insightful reading of early drafts of *Stage Directing*. All made significant suggestions for revisions and additions. For their important contributions to this book, I especially wish to acknowledge Elbin Cleveland for his interpretation of the floor plans of three Broadway plays and for the photographs of white models, Tim Donahue for graphic contributions, and Chet Goff for the many line drawings of figures and scenes from plays. The cover photographs (from a production of *Vanities* at Columbia College, Columbia, South Carolina) are by Tim Donahue, who also designed the cover for *Stage Directing*.

All of the production photographs are of plays produced at the University of South Carolina (USC). Photos are courtesy of USC's University Technology Support unit. The drawings for the productions of *As You Like It* and *Ghosts* are by Dennis C. Maulden, of the Flat Rock Playhouse. Jim Hunter designed the ground plan for *You Can't Take It With You*. *Mae and Her Stories* and *Cha-Cha-Cha* are printed with the permission of their respective authors, David DeWitt and Garth Wingfield. The drawing for *The Play About the Baby* was based on a photograph by Carol Rosegg; the drawing for *The Iceman Cometh* was based on a photograph by Joan Marcus. Each photographer gave permission to have their photo used as the basis for a line drawing.

This text is dedicated to Tim Donahue in acknowledgment of his patient guidance through the conception and writing of *Stage Directing: The First Experiences*.

The Director at Work

The director goes through at least six major steps in mounting a production. A script must be selected, studied, conceived, cast, rehearsed, and then performed. After the performance, there will be reactions to the performance either in a newspaper, in study groups, from friends, or perhaps from a mentor. Knowing these steps in advance will give the beginning director a way to approach the first directing experiences. The six-step directing process forms the organizational framework for the chapters that follow.

■ OVERVIEW

Collaboration is at the heart of theatrical production. Playwright, director, actors, designers, and audience all join forces to create a production performed live at a specific time and place. The director is the acknowledged leader of this collaborative process.

It is clear that actors, playwrights, and designers differ widely in their abilities, talents, and approaches to their specific crafts. So do directors. Some directors are recognized as world leaders in their field who almost always lead their collaborators to success in the theatre. Other directors are often inspired and occasionally have important successes, and still others are recognized as competent. What, then, distinguishes the competent journeyperson director from the true artist?

The Artisan-Director

Although not every director is equally talented in all aspects of the directorial process, each must become a highly proficient artisan if the production is to succeed with an audience. Every director is obligated to master the skills needed to collaborate effectively with actors and designers. The artisan-director is obligated to become an adroit craftsperson with the ability to devise a production concept that serves a particular audience at a particular time in a specific venue. This artisan-director must select an appropriate playscript, provide leadership to the designers, cast appropriate actors, guide their interpretation of the playscript, stage the dramatic action so that the production is efficiently served, and then rehearse the production. These skills, the focus of this book, can be honed. Their mastery depends not on native talent, but on study, hard work, and practice.

The Artist-Director

Exceptional directors have a generous imagination, an innate talent, a heightened sensitivity to understand and appreciate human emotions, a gift for collaboration, and a tolerance for anxiety. These people, artist-directors, expose themselves to music, art, politics, history, and nondramatic literature along the way, finding the resources of intellect and artistry to deepen their vision of theatre. The artist-director is fully skilled in the craft of directing; however the vision of this person goes beyond competence. This director is able to bring to the production a unique vision characterized by originality, passion, completeness of execution, and the ability to gather the best actors and designers with whom to collaborate. The artist-director is rare indeed, but aspiring to that title is a goal that may be undertaken with study and practice.

▰ GOALS

When you have read and studied this introduction, The Director at Work, you should be able to do the following:

- Distinguish between an artisan-director and an artist-director
- Describe the specific job of the director
- Explain some ways meaning is communicated nonverbally
- Identify directorial skills
- Delineate some directorial strategies
- Describe some copyright issues as they pertain to the director

▰ THE DIRECTOR'S JOB

The primary responsibility of the director is to organize and unify everything the audience sees and hears through time. The director must have a vision of the playscript that can be communicated to the audience through the means of sight, sound, and tempo. The director reads a script and develops a clear response to its emotional impact, meaning, and individuality of expression. The director must then communicate this conceptual understanding of the play by leading actors, designers, and others. Throughout the rehearsal period, the director serves as an ideal audience of one for the production company, giving feedback to the actors and designers. On opening night, the work of the director, actors, and designers comes together as a unified entity for the benefit of the audience.

The Audience Sees

The director must determine what the audience sees. Sets, lighting, and costuming, of course, constitute an important part of what the audience sees. But the actors' bodies and facial expressions also make a visual impact. The audience also sees the arrangement of the actors on the stage and their movements through the setting. Important, too, are the activities the actors engage in.

The Audience Hears

The director must manage what the audience hears. The actors speaking the playwright's words and the meaning the actors embody in those words are important parts of what the audience hears. Sound effects, both on- and offstage, also contribute to the sonic impact of the production. So does music. What the audience hears is influenced by how loudly or softly the actors speak and the timbre inherent in their voices or accents. Silence is also a significant aspect of the audience's auditory perception.

The Audience Perceives Time

The director must orchestrate the production through time. Unlike a novel or a poem that can be read and reread at leisure over long periods, a play unfolds entirely in the theatre through time at one sitting. Shaping what the audience sees and hears over time, then, is a third aspect of the director's responsibility. This production element is called *tempo*.

From the audience's view, the elements of sight, sound, and time must be unified in support of the production's meaning and its desired emotional impact. The unification and communication of these elements to an audience is the director's primary obligation.

▉ THE DIRECTOR AND MEANING

Another way to understand the director's job is to examine in additional detail how meaning is communicated in the theatre by visual means. Just as the words in the playscript connote and denote meaning, so do theatrical images—sets, lights, costumes, properties—as well as nonlinguistic sounds. The rate at which aural and visual sensations pass before the audience is also significant. Consider the several meanings associated with certain visual and aural stimuli.

- *Color.* Color has meaning. What does the color "red" signify? Does it signify only one meaning? Is the meaning of *red* different when it is the color of a dress worn by a specific character as opposed to the *red* of a fire hydrant?
- *Proximity.* The nearness or distance between people has meaning. If one character on one side of the stage says to another character, "I love you," but the listener is on the opposite side of the stage, then one meaning is conveyed. If they are entwined in an embrace, quite another spin is given to the words through proximity.
- *Pitch and volume.* How loud or soft a sound is communicated carries meaning. So does how high or low is the sound's pitch. This is true not only of linguistic sounds but of abstract and musical sounds. A whispered "I love you" conveys a meaning quite different from a shouted screechy "I love you." The words are the same but the meanings imparted are quite different.
- *Objects.* Items on stage or something that a character wears or handles transmit meaning. If a character wears dark horn-rimmed glasses, the audience

understands one meaning, but if that character wears outrageous "cat" glasses encrusted with rhinestones (as does Dame Edna, the drag character that Barry Humphries has created), then quite another meaning is communicated. At one time in our history, during the 1930s and 1940s, cigarette smoking was considered a sign of sophistication; today smoking conveys quite a different meaning. (See Figures 1 and 2).

■ *Space.* The theatre space and the stage space also communicate meaning. If the theatre building and audience space are quite upscale, say the Metropolitan Opera House in New York, one meaning (and expectation) is communicated to the audience attending the event in such a grand space. If the theatrical space is located in an industrial warehouse section of town and the audience is seated on bleachers, then quite another meaning is conveyed.

Savvy directors and designers are aware that meaning is communicated by all elements of the production, including the theatrical space, not just by the playwright's

words alone. Directors are now considered central to the production process because they are charged with unifying and distilling the many ways meaning is communicated to audiences.

▪ THE EFFECTIVE DIRECTOR

For a production to prosper, the director must manage the creative process with skill and sensitivity. To ensure that the director's vision is realized, certain specific abilities are demanded. The effective director must be able to do the following:

- Comprehend the structure and dramatic impact of a script
- Discern the intellectual thrust of a script
- Experience the impact of spoken dialogue
- Shape the pace of the production

(c)

FIGURE 1   Meaning. Three examples of smoking materials used to communicate quite different meanings. (a) The cigar smoker from *Death of a Salesman* suggests a crude, tough-minded business man who will fire Willy Loman from his sales position. (b) The scene from *Hedda Gabler* shows the title character smoking with Judge Brack, suggesting that she is quite a daring woman to smoke in public. (c) The manner in which the character from *The Glass Menagerie* holds his cigarette suggests a contemplative moment.

FIGURE 2   Costumes and Props Convey Meaning. The costume, glasses, and the way the cigarette is smoked reveal much about the standing female character in this scene from Lanford Wilson's *Fifth of July.* Notice her shoes and shorts: What do they say about the wearer?

- Inspire the designers and actors to make their best contributions
- Understand color, form, mass, and line
- Organize the creative team and the rehearsal process within the constraints of time and money
- Work well with a variety of personalities
- Define and solve problems as they arise during the production process

These are all daunting obligations. Some of the skills are partially tied to the personality of the director. Others can be developed through practice. The beginning director is not expected to master all of these qualities in the limited practical experiences one course can offer. Yet it is best if this director knows what eventually will be required to become proficient.

It is heartening to discover that not all experienced and successful directors master each skill with the same degree of success. For example, some directors turn out productions that are extraordinarily visual. Their stages are alive with color, movement, and exciting visual metaphors while the acting, perhaps, is only adequate. Other directors, as a result of the prominence of quite different directorial qualities, create productions that emphasize the script as a vehicle for extraordinary acting.

The strategy a director employs in developing a production often depends on those qualities, just outlined, that are the most highly developed in that particular director. It also relies on the director's background, special interests, and education.

No matter what the director's approach, realistically, the specific strategy must be based on the resources allotted to a specific production in a specific venue. It would be foolish for a director to depend on changing scenery by flying it if the theater did not have a fly loft. Or to rely on moving from scene to scene by rolling the scenery off stage on wagons if there is not adequate offstage space. Similarly, the beginning director would be unwise to select a script calling for seven male actors if they are not available. The director should realize that whatever strategy is employed, it must be forged within the specific constraints of the production circumstances.

■ DIRECTORIAL STRATEGIES

The director's overriding interpretation of a playscript that becomes the basis for the production is called a *directorial strategy*. This interpretation can be driven by a visual metaphor, a reconception of the playwright's specific circumstances (especially time and place), or it can be propelled by an intellectual/political slant toward the subject of the playscript. Some directorial strategies are quite shocking while others are quite straightforward. All directors definitely have a strategy, whether it is a conscious one or not. The way a director responds to a particular playscript reflects that director's unique view of the world, which will, perforce, reveal itself in the production.

No one particular directorial strategy is inherently better than another. If all directors interpreted a script in the same way, live theater would become stifling. Directorial strategies are best described as a continuum going from the very conservative to the seemingly brazen.

At one end of the continuum the directorial approach is *recreative*—directors see themselves as interpreters of the given text. This text-based approach to stage directing is analogous to conducting a symphony orchestra. The composer is the creative force while the conductor and instrumentalists are recreative artists charged with making what the composer wrote sound as compelling as possible. Using the recreative approach, the music can have great individuality from one recreation to the next, but all concerned are following the composer's intent.

At the other end of the continuum are stage directors who see themselves as *cocreators* of their productions, certainly equal with the playwright. These directors use the playwright's text only as a starting point for building stage productions. When this directorial strategy is employed, the audience may not quite recognize the text. (See Figure 3.)

The beginning director must understand the various approaches to stage direction that the contemporary theatre embraces. Student directors can better understand the art and craft of directing if they can place the stage productions they have seen (or will see) in a context.

FIGURE 3   Stage Sets Convey Meaning. While the time and place of Ibsen's *Ghosts* was not changed, it is clear that the director and designer wanted a setting that was neither naturalistic nor contemporary. This production concept emphasizes the eternal themes of *Ghosts,* not its period qualities. The hangings of translucent panels suggest the layers of the society in which the central character finds herself. The gossamer panels accommodated a strong expressionistic lighting effect at the climax of the play when a character is hallucinating and saying, "The light. Mother, the light."

Text-Centered Strategy

This strategy maintains that nothing should stand in the way of the script as the playwright wrote it. Text-centered directors conceive productions that they believe are true to the playwright's intention at the time of writing and thus accept the time and place as set forth by the author. This approach is basically recreative. If the playwright set the play in Oslo in 1888, then the sets, costumes, and props will reflect these particular circumstances. These recreative directors might even employ the theatrical traditions prevalent in 1888 Norway.

Recreative productions are often staged without cuts, with male roles played by males, and with no attention given to ethnic diversity in casting. By choice, the hand of the director is seldom discernible.

Gerald Gutierrez, for example, recently directed Edward Albee's *A Delicate Balance* brilliantly on Broadway guided by a text-centered strategy. The production was a straightforward rendition of the text with a group of exceptional actors who were able to illuminate the author's intentions. Critics found the production to be savagely funny, intensely moving, and dense with meaning. The director's contribution was hidden since audiences thought they were experiencing Albee's genius untouched by a unique directorial vision. All of the actors were giving performances that were touchstones of their careers and of the actor's craft. Three were nominated for Tony Awards.

Although the director's hand seemed invisible, the results showed Gutierrez's strategy at work. The actors were cast in roles each was uniquely suited to play; many were considered Broadway stars. Their styles, pacing, and interplay were balanced and assured. Audiences who had seen the original, highly acclaimed production of Albee's play in the late 1960s thought they never really knew before Gutierrez's 1996 production just how funny and moving the play could be. Clearly his directorial strategy was recreative and text-centered, his directorial hand all but invisible, yet the result was brilliant. Gutierrez won the best director Tony Award that year.

Director-Centered Strategy

This strategy, at the other end of the continuum, maintains that the director is a creator equal in importance to the playwright (see Figures 4 and 5). Director-centered

FIGURE 4   Casting and Design Convey Meaning. The director and designers chose to place this production of Shakespeare's *Romeo and Juliet* in a nonliteral platformed space with modern costumes. (a) A three-dimensional moon was used to underscore the language of the play in which "moon" and "night" are frequently referenced. The background was a neutral drop that changed color depending on how it was lighted. (b) To heighten the impact of the feud between the families, Juliet's family was cast with Caucasian actors and Romeo's with African American actors.

Text-Centered Strategy   Director-Centered Strategy

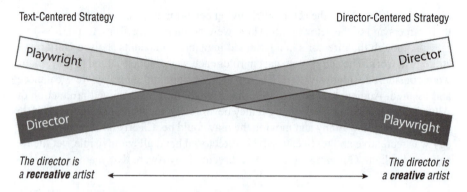

The director is
a *recreative* artist ←——————————————————————→ The director is
a *creative* artist

FIGURE 5   The Directing Strategy Continuum. Traditionally, the theatre director has been a recreative artist, functioning very much like a symphony conductor. The director, like the conductor, coordinates and unifies the work of other recreative artists. In theatre, this means actors and designers; in music, the instrumentalists. The goal of both leaders is to offer an interpretation of the creative artist, either the playwright or the composer. As the director's strategy has moved from the recreative to the creative, the director has, at the furthest edge of this continuum, become a creator equal in impact with the playwright.

productions use the playwright's text as the starting point for a new theatre experience; the words are among the least important features. A director-centered production may be characterized by theatrical or textual interpolations, cross-gender and/or color blind casting, and striking visual images that may or may not illuminate the text. The director is a co-creator of the production.

The acting in the director-centered production may be just as vivid and exciting as in the text-centered production, but other enhancements are included to help the audience understand and more fully appreciate the theatrical experience. The director might impose an extraordinary rhythm on the production that in and of itself excites the audience. There may be aural enhancements, such as expressionistic sound effects or surreal musical bridges, that are not triggered directly by the text. These enrichments, the director maintains, express the emotional core of the play in this time and place (see Figure 6 for an example).

An internationally respected director, Peter Brook, recently brought his production of *Hamlet* to New York. Shakespeare's four-and-a-half-hour script with just under thirty named characters was played in two-and-a-half-hours by eight actors playing thirteen roles. Scenes were rearranged, characters eliminated, and language simplified. Clearly Brook took a director-centered approach to what many consider to be the most important play in the English language. It is generally in revivals of playscripts in the public domain that director-centered productions are most prevalent.

The recent reinterpretation of J. B. Priestly's *An Inspector Calls,* produced with the blessing of the Priestly estate, is a telling example of this strategy. Priestly's work is a play of ideas in the guise of a drawing-room mystery written near the end of World

FIGURE 6   Director-Centered Strategy. The strategy for this production of
Aristophanes' *The Birds* was director-centered. The director became an adapter/
writer who, with his coadapter and composer, turned the Greek comedy into a
musical with heavy emphasis on spectacle. The king and queen of the birds, Procne
and Epops, for example, were played by dancers trained in ballet who could also act
and sing. Notice the costuming. The Aristophanes text was completely revamped
and considerably shortened, while the music followed models set by Mendelssonn,
Copland, Ravel, and Saint-Saens. There were no issues of copyright because the
coadaptors worked from a translation in the public domain.

War II and set slightly before World War I. The director, Stephen Daldry, and his designer, Ian MacNeil, set the play in a surreal space. A large doll house, raised off the
stage floor by stilts, occupied centerstage, and as the play began, the characters could
be seen and vaguely heard through the windows having a dinner party. About them was
fog and detritus, a ruined civilization. A silent chorus of dispossessed people emerged
from the orchestra pit and wings, hovering around the edges of the stage much of the
time. Because of air-raid sirens, the arrival of the urchins, and a misting rain that fell
on them, much of the opening dialogue was not heard and even less was understood.

After the initial scenes, the doll house shifted open and the characters de-
scended from it. A great deal of the production was staged in front of the house. The
acting style was not contemporary—the actors played no subtext but fully expressed
their actions as written. At one climactic moment, when the family is held responsible for the death of a young woman, the stilts on which the house sat shifted and
seemed to collapse. The house tilted forward and everything loose in it—china,
lamps, furniture—clattered onto the stage floor as the house collapsed. As the very

foundations of the family were shattered, so the very foundation of their house collapsed. When the family began to rationalize the young woman's death, the house magically began to right itself. Daltry's production lasted about one-hour-and-forty minutes without intermission.

This production would have been unthinkable in Priestly's time. Yet Priestly's play as written could hardly be successfully mounted in a contemporary theater today for it is truly old-fashioned. This production gave the playscript a second life as a nightmarelike production without changing a word of dialogue. It ran for nearly six years in London and eighteen months on Broadway. It became the most honored revival in the past twenty-five years, winning nineteen major awards including Tony Awards in 1994 for best revival of a play and for best direction.

Director-centered productions, such as Steven Daltry's reconception of *An Inspector Calls,* are not new to our era of theatre. Less than eighty years after Shakespeare's death, productions of *Romeo and Juliet* ended with the title characters alive and married. *King Lear* ended happily. Clearly these productions were rewritten with the thought of making them more accessible to a particular audience at a particular time. A much praised and respected recent New York, production of *Romeo and Juliet* called *R & J,* featured only four male actors in modern, neutral costume. Juliet was played by a male as was the Nurse. Further, lines from *A Midsummer Night's Dream* were interpolated into the script. The overriding concept for this version of *Romeo and Juliet* was that a quartet of the students in an all-male prep school were studying the play and what followed was a dreamlike interpretation of Shakespeare's play.

A Continuum

While some few directors are at the extreme ends of the directorial strategy continuum, most directors employ a production strategy that can be placed somewhere between the extremes of the text-based approach and the director-based tactic. These directors maintain that in order to make a playscript written in another era meaningful for today's audience certain adjustments in the text must be made but that the playscript must remain the recognizable work of the author. So the director frequently changes the time and place the author has specified. The script may be considerably shortened, arcane words might be altered, and the sequence of scenes might be reshuffled. The play's original meaning may be purposely distorted by the director to provoke more vigorous argument, to hold up the work for critical reappraisal, or to speak more forcefully to a contemporary audience.

In short, most directors follow a text-based strategy or a director-based strategy without finding themselves at the extreme in either direction.

The Universal Strategist

Unusual directors can, over a career, employ more than one of these strategies depending on the play, the venue, and the resources. For example, venerated twentieth-century British director Tyrone Guthrie was capable of mounting effective text-centered productions of Chekhov. His version of both parts of Marlowe's rather long *Tamburlaine the Great,* however, played on Broadway (1956) in under three hours with roles eliminated or combined and whole scenes cut or condensed. Later he directed *The House of Atreus,* a retelling of Aeschylus' *Oresteia* trilogy, at the theatre named for Guthrie in Minneapolis. The production used masks, a chorus, and some puppet-like costumes and took approximately three-and-a-half hours to perform. Clearly the last two productions were director-centered.

Your Directorial Approach

What will be *your* directorial strategy? You don't have to know the answer to this question immediately. You may begin your directing studies as a quite conventional strategist and emerge a director-centered tactician, or perhaps a universal strategist. (See Figure 7).

Whatever your directorial approach, your responsibility is to endow the production with a sense of reality—of unity, authenticity, and truth. No matter what the outward look of the production, its interior must yield some truth, however small it may be. The truth can be dramatic, emotional, erotic, or ornamental; however, that core of truth cannot be absent if the production is to have theatrical reality.

Don't confuse reality with realism. Realism is but one among many theatrical styles—expressionism, romanticism, classicism, and so on. Reality in this specific

FIGURE 7   Universal Strategy. The director who is a universal strategist finds plays from all periods to stage, including classics of the English theatre such as Sheridan's *School for Scandal* shown here.

FIGURE 8   Staging and Strategy. If the only standard is realism, this moment from a production of Noel Coward's *Private Lives* would never occur. Four people on a sofa might have similar facial expressions but probably they would not all be making the same gesture in the same manner at the same time. It is the director who shapes the actors' movements and expressions to suit the directorial strategy for a given play.

instance is that sense of truth that allows the playscript to communicate the here and the now to an audience (see Figure 8). To accomplish this goal, you will need the skills discussed at the beginning of this introduction to successfully express your vision of a playscript's reality through the work of actors, musicians, and designers.

NEW PLAYS

There are no established production conventions for new playscripts. The director of the first production of a play, in a truly collaborative relationship with the playwright, may greatly influence the writer to make additions and cuts and even to ask for new directions in the plot. The type of collaboration varies from director to playwright to production situation. The director of a new play can help guide the author to sharpen storytelling or clarify character, but alterations are made at the author's discretion and belong to the author.

It can be frustrating, exhilarating, and/or contentious because the roles of director and playwright, though they may be defined by contract and by the standards of their respective unions, are in reality fluid. But no matter, a good first production may well define what is a text-centered strategy for later generations of directors.

Elia Kazan had an enormous impact on Tennessee Williams's playscripts, especially in the production of *Cat on a Hot Tin Roof.* A central character, Big Daddy, died at the end of the second act in Williams's original version of the play. Kazan persuaded Williams to keep Big Daddy alive and to rewrite the third act. Williams took Kazan's suggestion and the version of the play that is almost universally produced fifty years later is the Broadway version directed by Kazan.

With Kazan's urging, the production of Arthur Miller's *Death of a Salesman* was greatly influenced by the setting suggested by designer Jo Mielziner. Miller had originally envisioned a system of stage wagons that would roll on and off to change scenes. Mielziner envisioned a permanent unit set that showed several rooms of the house and provided other acting areas downstage right and left. Miller was convinced and the printed edition describes the Mielziner concept.

Joshua Logan, the director of *South Pacific,* made so many contributions to the story of that now legendary musical that he was finally awarded coauthor credit with Oscar Hammerstein II. Later, during preproduction conferences and rehearsals, Logan persuaded William Inge to greatly alter the shape of *Picnic,* a drama headed for Broadway. Inge took Logan's advice and incorporated those suggestions; they are now part of the established script. The play was a huge hit and later was made into a highly successful movie.

A full exploration of theatrical style—current and historical—can be a life-long pursuit. This section has sketched one framework for understanding current staging strategies. Even if the student never directs again, knowing something about directorial approaches will enrich theatre-going and one's appreciation of other dramatic media, including television and film.

▬ COPYRIGHTS

Some forms of intellectual property, including playscripts, are protected by the government through the issuance of a *copyright,* which is a license granted to the author to control the dissemination of the work and to profit from it as the author sees fit. Whereas in the United States at one time, copyrights had to be applied for, current law grants copyright rights for any expression cast in a permanent form.

With works that have a copyright, permission from the author or an author's agent must be obtained in advance; and, usually, a royalty must be paid whenever the work is to be performed. Directors who alter copyrighted works for performances without the author's permission violate the contract with the author and put their producing organization at risk.

Moreover, the royalty agreement obligates the producing organization to perform the work "as written" (or, in the language which was used more often in the past, "substantially as written"). Playwrights have received court injunctions to halt productions that violate this clause of a licensing agreement.

Works in the public domain do not have copyrights. Public domain (a legal term) works are either ones for which the author has expressly given up the copyright or works for which a copyright has expired. The length of time a copyright is effective has changed over time, so determining whether a work is in the public domain can be somewhat complicated. At present, a U.S. copyright is valid for the life of the author plus seventy-five years.

Works in the public domain are fair "game" for any producing organization. They can be performed without payment of royalties, and scripts can be modified in any way the producing organization wishes.

▄▄ EXPERIENCES

Reading

Begin reading plays with the aim of selecting several as possibilities for class directing projects. A list of anthologies of short plays can be found in the Preface to this book. The more plays you have read, the more efficiently you will be able to make final decisions when that moment comes.

Meaning

Attend a local theatre production to note the ways in which nonverbal meaning is communicated. Were the things the actors handled effectively selected and used? Did their onstage activities reveal character? How? How not?

Look at a television network or cable drama with the sound off and observe how nonverbal meaning is communicated. Bring these observations to class and discuss them with your classmates.

Strategy

What directorial strategy seemed to govern the stage production you attended? Why?

▄▄ KEY TERMS

With sufficient study of this prologue, The Director at Work, you should be able to fully define the following terms:

- Artisan-director
- Artist-director
- Copyright
- Director-centered strategy
- Directorial skills

- Director's job
- Nonverbal meaning: color, proximity, pitch and volume, objects, space
- Text-centered directorial strategy
- Universal strategy

▀▀▀ WEB CONNECTIONS FOR MORE . . .

Suggestions for discovering more information about directing on the World Wide Web have been strategically placed at the end of each of the six major steps in the directing process. While almost all students perform internet searches the URLs cited can specifically expand and supplement the material found in each directing step.

These following Web sites will help you understand more about directing and plays available for production:

- The Society of Stage Directors and Choreographers is the union of professional directors and choreographers. To find out more about the directing profession, log onto www.ssdc.org. In particular, click on Membership to discover how one can join SSDC and click on Contracts to understand the extent of their jurisdiction. You can also discover aspects of the business side of directing—how much directors are paid for work in various types of theatres, the royalty payments directors earn, and more.
- Using a search engine like Google, enter the term "copyright" and browse through the many choices you get to learn more about terms such as "fair use."

STEP

1

Selecting the Playscript

Selecting the playscript or agreeing to direct a playscript someone else has picked is the most important decision a director makes. In some production situations, especially in community and educational theatres, the director is free to select the playscript to be directed. In others, the playscript is offered to the director or is assigned. In any production situation, however, there is never enough time to change plays if the director becomes disenchanted with the material during rehearsals. The clock does not stop—it relentlessly ticks the countdown until opening. The director, then, should carefully examine the strengths and weaknesses of the playscript to discover if it can be successfully mounted under the specific production circumstances.

What criteria should be used for making such an important decision? First, the director should read many playscripts in order to discover one or two that might be suitable (see Figure 1.1). Read with a theatrical eye (as opposed to a literary critics' perspective) and the naivete of a child to discover the playscript's story, structure, characters, ideas, and emotional force. Even if the script is a known commodity, it should be read with freshness.

FIGURE 1.1 Casting Requirements. This moment from the Howard Davies production of Eugene O'Neill's *The Iceman Cometh,* starring Kevin Spacey, clearly demonstrates the large cast, mostly male, needed to produce this classic American drama. If the director can't cast the production with the mandated number of competent actors, then another script, which can be cast from the available acting pool, should be selected.

OVERVIEW

At least seven areas should be explored when deciding the suitibility of a playscript for a specific audience in a specific performance space. These include the script's intrinsic dramatic merit, the director's personal and intuitive response to the playscript, its suitability for the specific producing organization and its audience, the resources that need to be made available for the production, the technical requirements of the script (see Figure 1.2), the availability of appropriate actors, and the licensing restrictions.

GOALS

You should be able to evaluate the strengths and weaknesses of a playscript for production in a specific theatrical space by using the checklist that follows.

PLAY SELECTION CHECKLIST

Does the Director Like the Playscript?
Whether the director can connect emotionally and intellectually with the playscript is at the heart of the selection process. The director should be excited by the prospect of giving theatrical life to the playwright's words and eager to face the challenges of the script.

FIGURE 1.2 Special Needs. George Bernard Shaw's *Misalliance* can be a satisfying directing experience if it can be effectively cast. Ages are important to the dramatic action and at least one character, whom Shaw has named "Bunny," must be diminutive for the comedy to work. Then, too, an airplane must crash into the conservatory (note the wing of the plane in the upper-right corner).

Some specific questions to consider: Does the director believe she can make this play come alive for an audience? Does the director feel comfortable with and even admire the values inherent in the playscript? Are the play's emotional tone and its meaning important to the director? Are the characters the author has chosen compelling? Is there an aspect of the script—idea, character, language—that the director would like to explore during rehearsals? In short, is the director fascinated by the prospect of directing this play?

Do the Playscript's Inherent Strengths Outweigh Its Weaknesses?

No script is perfect. Make a list of its strong points in one column and in a second column note its deficits. Use your personal judgment. Will the script's strong contemporary appeal, for example, be outweighed by its difficult language? Is the beginning too weakened by excessive exposition, or will this slowness be compensated for by a dynamic middle and an explosive climax? In short, the director asks if the script is stageworthy. This kind of analysis is practical and sobering.

Is the Playscript Suitable for Those That Will Most Likely See It?

Unlike the poet or painter who can work in privacy, theatre performance is inherently social. A play will not involve and move an audience that is too shocked by language, situation, or nudity to listen or care. Note that situation and language can refer to things other than sexuality and profanity. Violence, nihilism, criminality, extreme disrespect, and other things can also shock an audience.

Shocking language, situation, or nudity may be integral to a playscript's meaning and story, still the playscript may not be appropriate for all audiences. The language acceptable in the commercial theatre is probably not appropriate in a classroom where the audience has no choice but to attend. Obviously, plays aimed primarily at children must consider the limits of what is appropriate at various ages.

Some directors, for example, may be drawn by the complexity of D. H. Hwang's *M. Butterfly*—the story revolves around a diplomat's affair with a beautiful and graceful performer whom he discovers, rather late in their sexual relationship, to be a man. The play requires male frontal nudity. If the audience for *M. Butterfly* is quite conservative and reserved, they might not enjoy the production, no matter what its merits. Further, they may well become alienated from the producing organization. When in doubt, the director should consult the producer or the theatre board before proceeding.

Can the Playscript Be Effectively Directed in the Production Circumstances?

Some projects require more time to ready than others and some actors will require more rehearsals than others. Is there sufficient time to cast actors and rehearse them sufficiently? Is there sufficient money to successfully mount this playscript using the director's production scheme? Can the scenic effects and costumes be built in time for sufficient rehearsals to acquaint the actors with the environment and clothing?

The answer to these questions will, of course, depend on the director's approach to the script. But if the concept demands more time and money than the production circumstances can provide, the director should continue looking for a more stage-worthy script.

Can the Playscript Be Successfully Presented in the Intended Space?

Some scripts make specific demands that cannot be met by all theatres (see Figure 1.3). Is there enough onstage space to accommodate the number of characters required by the playscript to be on stage at one time? If a trap door is required, does the theatre have one? In one recent backstage farce, for example, a climactic scene requires an actor who is quite drunk to fall off the stage and into the theatre's orchestra pit. If the intended space has no orchestra pit and the director cannot see another solution to this blocking problem, it might be best to continue the search for an appropriate script.

Can the Playscript Be Cast Effectively?

Since every play presents its own set of casting problems, are actors with sufficient skill and emotional accessibility available for this production? If a sixty-year-old male character is required and an actor of sufficient age is not available, the director must look for another play. The director must not overestimate her ability and the ability of a twenty-year-old actor to play the part convincingly. The director and the actor will probably get so caught up in trying to act the age that there will not be time or energy to act the play.

There is no use, for example, in selecting and preparing to direct a seven-character, all-male play if seven competent male actors cannot be cast. Can some of the roles be played by females? If not, the director must continue searching for a more castable vehicle.

Is the Playscript Available for Production?

According to copyright laws, the playwright owns the playscript. Unauthorized or unlicensed productions are illegal. Theatres must first acquire the rights, called a *license,*

TIP: Make Notes

A director's first impressions of a playscript can be very telling. After a first reading, make a few notes to remind you later what impressed you or didn't impress you. Your remarks are for your eyes only, and thus can be in your particular shorthand. Complete sentences are not required, only the record of your very first reactions. You might note, "Marching band, but why? Think about this."

You might want to make notes on images the play conjured. Did you think of tex-tures, colors, current events? Notes might include, "Desert sand feeling. Why?" or, "Stock market scams!"

The notes might include some impressions of what is strong about the script. Or what might be some drawbacks to production, using the guidelines just posed. Again, make a list and be as specific as you can.

First impressions can be lasting ones, but only if you remember them!

FIGURE 1.3 Transformations. (a) Steve Martin's *Picasso at the Lapin Agile* makes a number of technical demands. The painting on the wall must disappear in the blink of an eye and be replaced by another. (b) A visitor from the future, someone very much like Elvis Presley, must magically appear accompanied by a burst of smoke. (c) At the play's climax, the set must somehow magically open to reveal the infinite universe that Albert Einstein, another character in the play, envisions. If the theatre in which this play is to be produced cannot accomplish these transformations effectively, then another script must be selected for production.

from the author's designated agent in order to produce a specific script. Current and recent Broadway and Off-Broadway successes are usually not licensed immediately for amateur production; their rights are restricted to road companies, regional theatres, and other professional venues. Only after these demands are exhausted will the script be released for school and community use.

However, the playscript, or a part of it, can be used for educational purposes in the classroom under the "fair use" clause of the current copyright law. This exception means that when the playscript is used exclusively for classroom exercises during the teaching of a course, the material can be performed in that circumstance without license.

ASSESSMENT

If the answers to any of the preceding questions are negative, the best advice for the director is to look for another script.

Sometimes the director is asked to direct a specific script with a specific group of actors in a specific theatre. This situation usually occurs in professional regional theatres where the artistic director has programmed a season of playscripts for production. The director must still determine if the playscript is one she feels comfortable directing after evaluating it using the guidelines just discussed and others. If not, the best advice is to turn down the invitation to direct.

EXPERIENCES

Making Choices: The Directing Projects
During the course of the term, you will be asked to select, cast, and direct several projects. From the plays you have been asked to read, select several that interest you, then choose three or four on the basis of the checklist in this chapter. Duplicate each of the plays for reference and analysis during Step Two of this book.

Script Evaluation
Select a script you are interested in directing. Use a strengths/weaknesses chart similar to the one shown in Figure 1.4 to evaluate the stage worthiness of a playscript.

WEB CONNECTIONS FOR MORE . . .

These Web sites will help you understand more about Selecting the Playscript.

■ To learn more about the organization of American playwrights, the Dramatists Guild of America, log on to *www.dramaguild.com.* Especially browse Theater Links to find out which plays various theatres have scheduled for production and *The Dramatist Magazine,* which features certain articles from their publication free of charge.

FIGURE 1.4 Keep Score.

Play's Strengths	Play's Weaknesses

Conclusion:

- Using a search engine like Google, enter the term "ten-minute plays" and browse through some of the sites. You will be led to booksellers who stock anthologies of these short plays as well as to the sites of specific authors of ten-minute plays, which can be downloaded free of charge.
- Use the following URLs to see how important regional theatres curate a season of plays:
    Actors Theatre of Louisville—*www.actorstheatre.org*
    Alliance Theatre Company (Atlanta)—*www.alliancetheatre.org*
    Alley Theatre (Houston)—*www.alleytheatre.com*
    Lincoln Center Theater (New York City)—*www.lct.org*
    Roundabout Theatre Company (New York City)—*www.roundabouttheatre.org*
    Seattle Repertory Theatre—*www.seattlerep.org*
    South Coast Repertory (California)—*www.scr.org*
    Williamstown Theatre Festival (Massachusetts)—*www.wtfestival.org*
- If you are looking for playscripts or musical plays, the following websites will be useful in helping you learn more about specific scripts. These site lists the plays that each organization or company can license, giving a brief synopsis of the script, the author, the number of male and female characters, staging requirements, and royalty information. Many licensing agencies sell copies of scripts online.
    Dramatists Play Service—*www.dramatists.com*
    Dramatic Publishing Company—*www.dramaticpublishing.com*
    Broadway Play Publishing—*www.broadwayplaypub.com*
    Samuel French Inc.—*www.samuelfrench.com* (This site only allows you to buy scripts; it does not now give summary information.)
    Music Theater International—*www.mtishows.com*
    Tams-Witmark Music Library—*www.tamswitmark.com*
    Rodgers and Hammerstein Theatre Library: *www.rnh.com*

2 Analyzing and Researching the Playscript

A playscript creates a unique situation, usually with strongly opposed forces, and it usually develops rising tension over time. When a playscript is acted before an audience in the theatre, its effect may be analyzed from three perspectives: emotional impact, intellectual meaning, and personality.

The playscript's *emotional impact* is perhaps the most obvious of these qualities. Do we laugh, cry, cringe? Do we feel anger, wonder, pity, anguish, fear, relief? Are we puzzled? Mystified?

The playscript's *meaning* is its intellectual effect on an audience. It encompasses the playscript's ethical, political, or social values; insight into human psychology; and the judgment or compassion of the work. Do we understand the core meaning we have seen? Are the values in the play ones we endorse? Reject? Or do we see in the production cultural folly?

The playscript's *personality* is the author's unique manner of expression. Is the playscript passionate or ironic? Humorous or dramatic? Is the story told in a linear manner? Are the characters motivated by psychology? Do the characters speak in the language of the street or in a language that could exist only in literature? Does the play use the conventions of an established genres, such as farce, romantic comedy, absurdism, expressionism, and so on, or is the shape less predictable? The author's personality is manifested not only by the playscript's emotional impact and meaning but also by the playwright's manner of expression.

The most effective production of any playscript, of course, is one in which the *emotional impact, meaning,* and *personality* are inseparable. Each affects the others and is interwoven with the others. The play in performance, in this case, is one in which the director has unified these elements to give the audience an artfully sustained experience.

Discovering the emotional impact, meaning, and personality of a playscript is not a magical process, nor is it an entirely intuitive one. It requires study and analysis, particularly of the dialogue. The director can discover almost everything there is to know about a playscript through a careful investigation of its dialogue. The saying "Plays talk, movies show" is quite accurate. While the author's stage directions and notes may be helpful to the director and actors, it is what the characters say that unlocks the play's people, its plot and core meaning, and the author's individuality.

■ OVERVIEW

The four major sections of this chapter are devoted to dissecting the playscript in order to discover its mechanisms. Only when the director clearly understands the plot and how its incidents are structured, the people and their individual traits, and the playscript's core meaning is it possible to make artistic decisions that will bring the script to life on stage and reveal its inherent qualities to the audience. Researching the script will broaden the director's knowledge about the era in which it is set and the specific references in the playscript that may be unknown to the director (see Figure 2.1).

How Plays Are Made

Playscripts can be structured in many ways. Even a casual examination of *Happy Days, Baltimore Waltz* or *A Raisin in the Sun* will reveal structural diversity. The most common structure, however, is *cause-and-effect*—one incident leads logically and linearly to the next. Most modern realistic drama follows this organizational structure. It is exemplified admirably by Lorraine Hansberry's *A Raisin in the Sun,* Tennessee Williams's *A Streetcar Named Desire,* and Arthur Miller's *Death of a Salesman.*

FIGURE 2.1   Research. John Olive's *The Voice of the Prairie* is set in middle America during the early days of radio. Not only must the designers research these given circumstances, but the director must know what this era was like so that the props and the costumes can be handled with authority. Note the use of strawhat, bow tie, and microphone.

Other plays are organized by the playwright's ideas. In this structure, one idea is linked somehow to the ideas that follow. Samuel Beckett's *Happy Days* eschews causality and is organized by its ideas.

Still, other plays are episodic in structure. In many of the plays of Bertolt Brecht, the episodes are interspersed with song and direct address. The postmodern plays of Paula Vogel, *Baltimore Waltz* and *How I Learned to Drive* for example, are not chronologically arranged nor are they linear. These playscripts seem to be held together by the internal life of the central character.

There are probably as many ways to structure a play as there are playwrights. But it's clear that the great preponderance of playscripts are organized causally. The discussions of script analysis that follow are based on a linear, causal plot structure. In fact, the beginning director is best served by first directing psychologically real, modern, linear playscripts. Once this structure has been experienced, other structures can be examined.

Read and Reread

Hardly anyone can read a play one time and, during that first encounter, discover enough about how the script is structured so that intelligent directoral decisions can be made. Multiple readings are required to determine a play's mechanisms, including core meaning, dramatic action, units, beats, given circumstances, and characters. Be prepared to read, reread, and read again, each time with a slightly different focus. Plan to read the play enough times to assimilate its world, to become familiar with its people, and to decipher its implications for production.

■■■ GOALS

When you have completed Step Two, you should be able to do the following:

- Chart the beginning, middle, and end of a playscript
- Identify a playscript's given circumstances
- Describe the difference between plot and story
- Understand the kinds of research that the script requires
- Distinguish between act, scene, unit, and beat
- Identify a French scene
- Explain the concept of actable verbs
- Identify action units
- Phrase objectives
- Discover a character's action, personality, and functional traits
- Construct a superobjective for each character
- Distinguish between action and meaning
- Create a statement of core meaning

▞▞ STRUCTURE

The heart of a modern realistic playscript is people in conflict. One form of conflict is interpersonal such as the disagreements between mother and daughter or boyfriend and girlfriend. In fact, the vast majority of American plays during the last century have been energized by domestic conflicts. Conflict sometimes pits an individual against some external force such as a governmental policy or law. These ideological conflicts still must be expressed as personal ones by the director. It is only through the character's personal involvement with the issues that the ideological conflict has emotional force. The director must understand the people of the playscript and recognize their conflict.

The way the conflict is arranged and developed by the playwright is called *plot.* A plot is specifically and progressively ordered by the playwright; it is not a random assortment of events in the majority of modern plays. The director must understand the playscript's plot—its structure for growth and shape.

There are several ways to investigate plot. One meaningful method for the beginning director is to divide the play into three sections—beginning, middle, and end— and study each section separately to discover how the play is organized. Analyzing a play in this simple way can be very useful in determining where the play is going and how it is getting there.

Discovering the playscript's structure is the director's most important homework assignment. Several readings of the script are required to understand fully what is happening to whom and why. All of this information is contained in the dialogue and sometimes in the playwright's notes. With each reading, the astute director will uncover more evidence of the playscript's unique world.

Beginning

The beginning of a play, of course, encompasses the first section of the playscript. Here the playwright sets forth the basic situation, introduces characters, sketches in the back-story (sometimes called antecedent action), and establishes the conflict/ tension that will become the heart of the action. This information is collectively called the play's *given circumstances.* Givens include the specific time and place of the action; the characters' social class, age, sex; and the prevailing mood/atmosphere of the situation. In short, these are the details provided by the playwright to help the actors create a world in which their characters function.

Given circumstances are uncovered primarily by a careful reading of the dialogue—what characters have to say about themselves and others. Sometimes this background information is called exposition; here it will be considered as the playscript's givens. While a majority of the given circumstances are set forth in the play's first section, certain other givens will continue to be revealed as the playscript unfolds. The playwright may also indicate given circumstances in the stage directions and notes concerning time and place.

The director must clearly understand the playscript's given circumstances because many decisions need to be based on this information. Specific givens will affect setting, casting, costuming, decor, and many other elements of a production.

Often, given circumstances are grouped as a series of Ws—when, where, what, and who. A fifth W, the why, is often discerned with the actors during the rehearsal process. Beginning directors probably have studied given circumstances in acting classes, but a short review from a director's perspective will be helpful. All too often actors and directors forgo this study as "too academic"; however, knowing the specific given circumstances clearly and in depth is a most useful key to unlocking the structure of a playscript.

Who? The People of the Play

The set of given circumstances includes the personal history of the characters and their relationships with one another. Age, sex, physical health, demeanor, and level in society all contribute to defining characters. An examination of the *who* will reveal the central character, called the *protagonist,* and his or her wants and needs. It will also identify who is preventing the protagonist from getting what is wanted; this character is called the *antagonist.* If the director can't identify these characters, she hasn't discovered the play's core conflict.

The other characters in the play are in one way or another connected to the antagonist or protagonist. These secondary characters serve a dramatic function by allowing the central characters to act on them by arguing with them, asking for their help, and/or providing them with needed information. Sometimes a secondary character represents the audience norm or the author's position in the conflict. Look for a fuller discussion of character in the Character section of this step.

TIP: Story versus Plot

All plays have a story as well as a plot. The saying, "a story has time to roam, a plot must stay at home," is very telling. Stories may be sprawling, rambling constructs, but plots are concentrated, distilled inventions.

Story is all-inclusive, suggesting a broader arc over time. A story is everything that happens over a broad, chronological time span. It is organized along the "this happened, and then that happened, and then something else happened" structure like a string of pearls on a necklace.

Plot is a highly selective form of story. It is the author's choice of only certain "pearls" from the story necklace. These selected events are then carefully arranged in the present tense to make some point. Plot is what happens on stage in the "here and now." Characters in a plot may talk about past events, but the action is always in the present tense.

The units in a story, its individual "pearls," can be arranged climactically or episodically. *Climactic* plots exhibit a cause-and-effect relationship that links the units by motive as in "because of this, therefore that." An *episodic* arrangement of units is much looser and does not necessarily follow a causal relationship. An episodic arrangement begins earlier in the story and includes more units, so the action is not as compressed as in a climactic arrangement. Shakespeare's plays use the episodic arrangement of story. Most television dramas use a climactic arrangement.

When? The Specific Time of the Action

This given circumstance includes the time, date, month, and year. The playwright may provide some of this information under a discussion of *setting*. If a specific time is not contained in the dialogue or notes, this omission might also be a clue to the nature of the playscript. Sometimes the director must invent this given to aid the designers and the actors. But, again, a careful reading of the script will reveal many more significant facts.

The *when* also includes the elapsed time of the play's sections. Some playscripts take place over an extended time span while others include no more time than it takes the play to unfold on stage. Elapsed time may be material to the plot. In other plays, elapsed time is unimportant to the plot.

Where? The Environment of the Playscript

The *where* includes the physical place of the action and reflects the social and economic background of the characters. The *place* includes the geographical locale: the neighborhood, city, state, and country. It also includes the exact place of the action be it a living room, a front porch, or a kitchen.

Exploring the *where* will lead to an understanding of the physical requirements of the setting, but *where* is more than a floor plan or set. It can include social groupings, societal influences, occupations, friendships, social standards, and family clusters, all of which illuminates the characters' background.

What? The Prior Events as Well as the Current Events of the Playscript

The *what* includes the major conflict that will become the heart of the playscript in performance and will be developed in the play's middle and end. The event that initiates the conflict, called the *inciting* incident, is also included in the *what*. It is important for the director to know what started it all. In many modern plays, the inciting incident occurs before the action has begun and is mentioned in the playscript's beginning section. In *Death of a Salesman,* for example, the inciting incident is Biff's return to the Loman home after an absence of several years. Before Biff's reappearance, there was an uneasy balance in the way Willy and Linda lived. Biff upsets this balance. The play begins shortly after Biff appears.

Middle

The middle section of a playscript is the development of the obstacles and complications that escalate the conflict/tension. Hence this element of structure is sometimes called *rising action.* In this second section of the play, additional background information may be revealed, but the thrust of the play's middle section is the development of a conflict. Incident is piled on incident in a generally escalating flow that leads to the climax and to the end of the action (see Figure 2.2).

Conflict also may be developed by the introduction of one or more subplots that involve secondary characters. Subplots usually mirror or contrast with the main action to expand the play's meaning or scope.

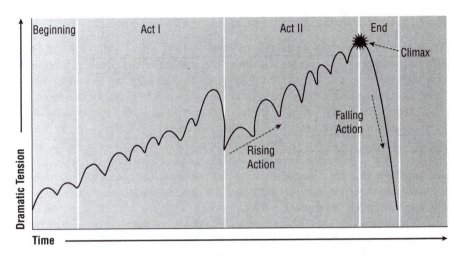

FIGURE 2.2   Rising and Falling Dramatic Tension in a Full-Length Play. This graph charts the rising tension of an imaginary two-act play. Note that as incidents accrete, the tension mounts until it is released at the climax.

Even a very short playscript may have several complications, which intensify its central action. Longer playscripts can have dozens of complicating incidents. Discovering these incidents, and learning when they begin, end, or overlap helps the director clarify and shape the forward action during rehearsal. (See Figure 2.3.)

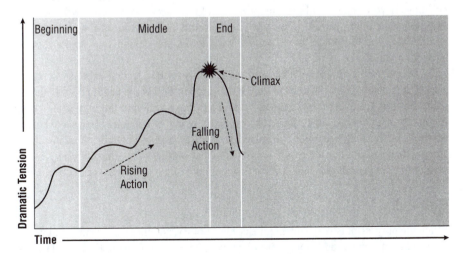

FIGURE 2.3   Rising and Falling Dramatic Tension in a Short Play. A short play occupies less time in the theatre, so the rising and falling action are briefer and less detailed than in longer plays.

End

The end of the playscript contains the climax and the falling action. Most modern plays move inexorably toward the definitive moment, called the *climax*. It is by far the most important structural element for the director to identify and to understand because all other incidents move toward and then fall away from this key moment.

The climax, in most plays, is the moment of explosion when the protagonist discovers something about herself or the world around her that forces her to see that world differently from then on. The climax, thus, is the moment of realization and/or change. If two or three central characters undergo this change, the one who changes last (most often) is the protagonist. If the director is unclear as to which character is the protagonist, identifying the climax and discovering who is most changed at that moment will clarify the matter.

The central character faces the mounting tension and suspense brought on by the complicating incidents and a decision is made. Tension is released. The action now will move in a different direction. The winding down of the play after the climax is called denouement or *falling action*. In modern plays, the falling action is the shortest section of the play.

Knowing Structure

The goal of plot analysis is to unlock a playscript's structure. Only by seeing how a playscript is made and understanding its discrete parts and how they are linked can the director fully comprehend the playscript's arc over time. Armed with this knowledge, the director is better able to clarify the action and stage the play with confidence.

Knowing the structure of a playscript is like having a blueprint for a proposed building. If you understand the blueprint, you know how the building will be built. The same is true of plays. If you clearly understand the structure of the playscript to be directed, you will know how to work with actors and designers to make it come alive for an audience.

Identifying a playscript's structure is not only an intellectual exercise in analysis, but it is also the foundation on which the director builds the production. If the director has not discovered the importance of a bit of exposition in the play's beginning section through analysis, then the actors probably won't give much emphasis to the exposition and the audience will be confused. If the director does not understand the play's climax, then perhaps the actors will toss it off as just another event; thus the play's major incident might be glossed over and the production may be judged as ineffective.

Research

When the playscript is very short, quite contemporary, and there are no unusual words or cultural references, additional research may not be called for (see Figure 2.4). Most longer scripts will require at least some research. For example, Neil Simon's *Biloxi Blues* makes reference to F. Scott Fitzgerald's *The Great Gatsby*. If the director does not know this landmark novel set in the 1920s and the character of Daisy Miller, he

(a)

(b)

FIGURE 2.4   Knowing What to Research. Thomas Gibbon's *Bee-Luther-Hatchie* is set in the present day. (a) One scene is placed in a bar, (b) another in a motel room. In an otherwise bare set, the two different sets of tables and chairs support the play's given circumstances. Because most of us have seen the bars and motels of today, little research is needed by the designers. The director, however, must research the contemporary implications of this unusual story.

will not be in a position to understand the conversation between the central character and the young girl he meets at a dance. Or, if the word *ignominy* is said by one character, the director must know its meaning and pronounciation in order to guide the actor effectively.

In David Rabe's *Streamers,* a group of men is slated to be shipped to Vietnam for active combat duty. The director must know the cultural and political significance of this war in southeast Asia. If the script is Arthur Miller's *The Crucible,* then surely the director must investigate the milieu of Salem and its witch trials in order to comprehend more clearly the given circumstances of the script.

Sometimes the playwright will warrant further investigation. When did Tennessee Williams live? How is his life reflected in *The Glass Menagerie*? Williams's biography is most certainly relevant to the world of this play.

The director, then, must know everything there is to know about the words in the script, and the world of the playwright if that knowledge is important to staging the script. The only way that understanding can be uncovered is through research.

Experiences

Analysis

Study the two short plays found in Appendixes A and B. Select one and divide it into a beginning, middle, and end; note the given circumstances in writing. Share your analysis with the group.

Determine, in writing, the climax of the play you selected. Share your analysis with the class.

Select a short play, which you will direct, for analysis in this and subsequent sections in Step Two. Divide it into a beginning, middle, and end; note the given circumstances in writing.

Research

In *Cha-Cha-Cha,* found in Appendix B, there are references that demand to be researched. Can you answer the following questions: What is *South Pacific*? Who is Bloody Mary? Why is it strange that Sheila played that role? Henry mentions Eames chairs and a Saarinen dining table. Can you find a picture of them to show your actors? Do you know Gloria Gaynor's hit recording of "I Will Survive"? Can you get a copy and play it for your actors? All of these questions can be answered by searching the Internet.

ACTS, UNITS, AND BEATS

Many playscripts are structured so that they move forward over time, to communicate that something is happening. That is, plays progress; they go somewhere; they grow. The events in a play are structured by the playwright so that what comes next is more interesting, more compelling than what preceded it. It may be brought about by the introduction of a new character, or a new twist in the plot, or it may be that the characters uncover new information that mandates change. Sometimes the growth is psychological. The playwright organizes the events with causal growth in mind.

The rate of progression, of course, is not constant. If it were, the play would seem as dull as if there were no growth at all. The incidents escalate, peak, and then recede as another incident repeats the ebb-and-flow action. This wavelike motion was graphed in the previous section, structures, as rising and falling action that moves through the playscript's beginning, middle, and end.

A playscript, however, can be broken down further. Starting with the smallest parts, a script is also made up of several dialogue exchanges called *beats*. A number of beats form a larger group called *units*. When units are combined, they form *scenes*.

Scenes combine to form *acts*. Several acts make a play. A novel is structured in a similar fashion. It has sentences, paragraphs, chapters, sections, and sometimes even larger parts called books.

Acts and Scenes

Long plays have been plotted to have as many as five acts or as few as one. Clearly, a five-act script has many more action units and takes longer to unfold in the theatre than does a one-act play.

Most contemporary full-length plays are now structured to have two acts. *Acts* are the most obvious and largest sections of the script since the author has clearly labeled them. An act can have several clearly marked scenes within it, also identified by the playwright.

Tennessee Williams arranged *A Streetcar Named Desire* into eleven scenes with two intermissions. But clearly *Streetcar,* which usually takes more than two-and-a-half hours to unfold in performance, has more than eleven action units in its plot.

Mary Chase's popular comedy, *Harvey,* has five scenes grouped into three acts. The first two acts each begin in the library of a large home and then move in the second scene to a sanatorium. The third act is set only in the sanatorium. Clearly this script has, by the author's plotting, five major divisions. The director is obligated to understand the structure of each of these scenes by dividing them further into action units.

Action Units

An *action unit* is an individual and separate section of a play that comprises one part of the dramatic action. If plot is the arrangement of the incidents, a unit is one of many discrete incidents. Each action unit may be independently dramatized, but taken together the incidents make up the plot. (See Figure 2.5).

Action units, then, are like the Roman numerals in an outline prepared for a public speaking class or for a research paper. The outline for a short speech may have one Roman numeral for the introduction, another for the body, and a third for the conclusion. Each Roman numeral identifies an independent (but related) section of the speech. The introduction is related to the body and the conclusion is related to the introduction and body. The same is true of plays. One Roman numeral is the beginning, the second is the middle, and the third numeral is the end section of a playscript.

Longer, more complicated outlines have a body that may encompass several main points, each represented by a Roman numeral. The same is true for plays. Longer plays have more action units than do shorter plays. A short play is usually made in one scene without a break in the action. Still, the author devises several action units in the arcing action.

Label Each Action Unit

Once the action units have been determined, a label, which describes the action within the unit, should be devised for each one. The label can be a complete sentence that

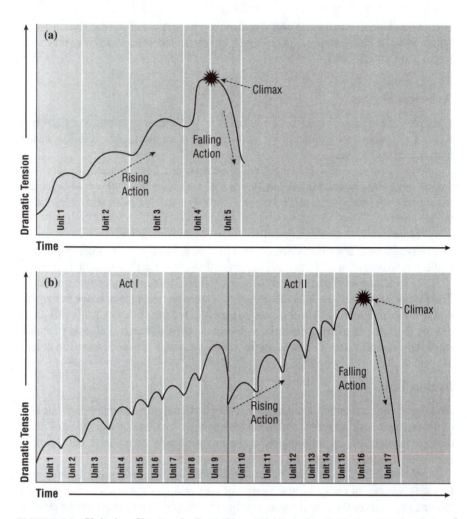

FIGURE 2.5   Units in a Short and a Long Play. The diagrams which charted rising and falling action have been further developed to illustrate how units make up the elements of a play's action. (a) The short play has five action units. (b) The longer play has seventeen units, divided into two acts with nine units in the first act and seven in the second. Clearly the two-act play has a more complicated plot and thus occupies more time in the theatre.

summarizes what happens in that unit ("Jane confronts Tom with the truth"), or it can be a phrase ("The confrontation"). Armed with this brief outline, the director can study the play's progression over time.

Note the phrasing of the action units in the box about *Brighton Beach Memoirs*. Here the director used complete sentences.

Action Units in Brighton Beach Memoirs

The first dozen action units in Act I are listed here. Using this model, you should be able to devise such a unit breakdown for the plays you will direct in class. It is not necessary to know this Neil Simon play to understand the nature of each action unit.

1. Eugene justifies his crazy family to us.
2. Nora craves to be in a Broadway show.
3. Nora and Laurie vow to buy Blanche a house.
4. Stan confesses to Eugene that "principle" may cost him his job.
5. Kate reminds Stan to ask for his pay early.
6. Blanche suffers an "attack" as Jack comes home.
7. Jack divulges to Kate he has lost one of his two jobs.
8. Eugene discovers he has a rival for Nora's affection.
9. Jack speculates whether Blanche will ever remarry.
10. Nora appeals for Stan's help; Stan seeks Nora's help.
11. The family deliberates over dinner (Eugene picks at but won't eat his liver; Jack urges Stan to ask for a raise; Blanche hints about Nora's job offer; Stan lays the groundwork with Jack; Jack lays the groundwork for more family; Nora forces a decision).
12. Nora pleads her case . . . (and so on).

Many of these units are clearly marked by the entrance and exit of characters or groups of characters. French scenes (see next section) in this play are significant indicators that one unit has concluded and another has begun.

French Scenes

Beginning with the playwright's breakdown of acts and scenes, a playscript can also be further subdivided into sections marked by the entrances and exits of characters. This method of breakdown is called *French scene analysis.* Dividing long plays into French scenes might be an intermediate step to help the director discover the distinct units of action.

Studying the French scene layout of a playscript can reveal much about its construction. Because a play is a *made* object, not life itself, people enter and exit for a reason, the playwright's reason. The author is signaling that one unit is over and another one is to begin.

A French scene can be made of one unit or it can be composed of several units. Only an examination of the play's dramatic action will determine how many action units are encompassed in a particular French scene. A French scene breakdown also is a useful device for scheduling rehearsals since the director can easily see which characters are needed to rehearse each scene.

Beats

An action unit can be further examined by identifying *beats*—the playscript's small-est measure of dramatic progression. An action unit is composed of several beats, while there are hundreds of beats in a long play (see Figure 2.6).

New beats can often be perceived easily and objectively. They are the precise moment when the subject of a conversation changes, a new topic is introduced, the in-tensity between characters changes, or the emotional tone shifts. In short, a beat is marked when a transition occurs.

A new beat is defined at that moment when the character's objective changes; that is, when a character's motivation changes, a new beat is declared by that change. For example, one character may want something this very moment from a second char-acter; the second character is reluctant to give it (first beat). So the first character tries another approach (the perceived transition) to get what she wants; the second charac-ter then gives in (second beat). This dramatic action is accomplished in two beats.

FIGURE 2.6   Acts, Scenes, Units, and Beats. A long play is made of acts, scenes, action units, and hundreds of beats. A short play will most likely be made in one scene with several units and numerous beats.

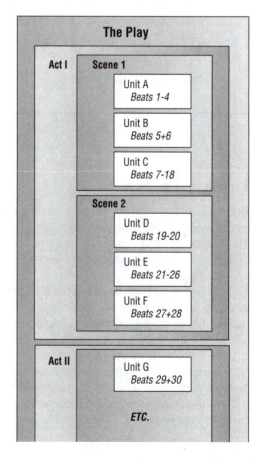

An analogy to music may be useful in understanding the relationship of action units and beats. In music, a measure is a group of related notes while a group of related measures is called a musical phrase. In drama, a series of sentences spoken in a scene makes up a beat, while a series of beats makes up an action unit.

Playwrights construct beats just as novelists construct paragraphs. However, in the playscript, there is no identifying indentation to alert the director or actor that one thought or action has concluded and another is to begin.

If you perceive a beat change, mark it by drawing a line across the script to separate one beat from the other. If you are newly aware of beats, don't stew over identifying beat changes; know that they are there and can be discovered and/or refined with additional study or during rehearsals. After a few experiences, you'll spot a beat change like it's second nature.

Objectives—The Why

An important reason to identify beats is to help the actor realize the character's every unique moment. Beats change when the character's objective changes. If there is a change in the dramatic action, the actor must act it in order to contribute to the playscript's forward movement.

An *objective* is phrased using an active verb to express what the character wants or needs at that particular moment in the playscript. For the objective to be most helpful to the actor, the verb should be stated in the imperative with the object of the verb identified in the phrase—thus, "Calm Mitch!" or "Demand the answer from Mitch this very minute!" Imperative verbs require action. The actor must pinpoint the transition from one objective to the next by making it specific and active. It is by acting on specific, playable objectives that the actor makes the character *do* rather than *be*— a passive, dull state. A specific example of how beats and objectives are used can be studied in the short playlet, *Waiting* by Tim Donahue, which follows this section.

In the discussion of given circumstances, the four Ws were identified: who, what, where, and when. Objectives (also called intentions) are the fifth W that make up the playscript's given circumstances. Objectives are the *why* and they encompass the character's moment-by-moment motivation.

Experiences

Waiting

The short vignette, *Waiting,* could be the beginning sketch for a two-act play, or it could be the basis of a substantial one-act play. Read it now in its present form without noting the comments in the second column. Then reread the vignette and observe how the playwright has marked and labeled its action units by reading the play along with the material in the second column. Do you understand why he divided the sections as he did? Do you agree? Why? Why not?

The first action unit has been further divided into beats. Complete the analysis by identifying the beats in the remaining units.

French Scenes in Ibsen's *Ghosts*

How well you know *Ghosts* is not important. The following analysis illustrates one way to break down the action in a play. Page numbers in the script used for this production are included in the analysis to suggest the length of the French scene.

Act I
1. Regine, Engstrand (5–11)
2. Regine, Manders (11–15)
3. Alving, Manders (15–24)
4. Alving, Manders, Osvald (24–30)
5. Alving, Manders (30–38)
6. Alving, Manders, Osvald, Regine (38–40)

Act II
7. Alving, Manders, Osvald, Regine (41)
8. Alving, Manders (41–49)
9. Engstrand, Manders (Alving listens) (49–57)

10. Osvald, Alving (57–64)
11. Osvald, Alving (64–67)
12. Osvald, Alving, Regine (67–69)
13. Alving, Manders, Osvald (69–71)

Act III
14. Alving, Regine (72)
15. Manders, Regine, Engstrand (72–74)
16. Alving, Manders, Engstrand, Regine (74–77)
17. Osvald, Alving, Regine (77–81)
18. Osvald, Alving (82–89)

By using this French scene breakdown, the director can readily see that there are at least eighteen action units over three acts in *Ghosts*. Some French scenes contain only one action unit (scene 14 is very short), while due to their length, others probably have several units (scenes 3, 4, 5, and 9 are longer).

TIP: Actable Verbs

Here are some verbs that beginning directors might want to include in their vocabularies. These verbs are filled with action that, if appropriately selected and fully played, can energize a beat.

admit, assault
beguile,
challenge, comfort
dazzle, defuse, delay, dominate
embarrass, enlist, entreat
fascinate, frighten
galvanize, goad, grant
hamper, harass, horrify, humiliate
implore, interest, intimidate
jab, jar, justify
keep, kill

lambast, lobby, lure
manipulate, mock, mollify
needle, negate, negotiate
obscure, order
pacify, pardon, plead
question, quit
restrain, retreat, reward
sacrifice, scold, shame, surrender
tantalize, tempt, torment, train
underscore, vilify
warn, wonder

Action Units

As a group, select and study one of the plays in the appendices. Divide the play into units. How many units did you discover? Share your analysis with the class. Is there agreement? Why? Why not?

Beats

Take one unit from the play you chose and divide it into beats. How many beats did you discover? Share your finding with the class. Is there agreement?

Objectives

Determine what objective each character is playing in each beat in the unit you are analyzing. Share this information with the class. Is there agreement?

Add ten actable verbs to the collection of verbs found in the Actable Verbs tip in this chapter.

French Scenes

Select a long play and divide it into French scenes using the example from *Ghosts* as a model.

Waiting

by Tim Donahue

Music from a portable tape player. The lights come up on an empty stage. JESSICA is dancing alone, practicing a dance routine. JESSICA is in seventh grade, a precocious twelve-year-old. She reaches up, twirls and falls. From the wings, we hear applause. JESSICA looks offstage.	**Unit 1: The Confrontation— Jessica attacks John for being late**
JESS: You're late.	
(JOHN, her brother, enters from offstage, still clapping and smirking. He is in eleventh grade and sixteen years old. JESS turns off the music.)	
JESS: You're late.	Beat 1
JOHN: You're very good.	Jess goads John for being late
JESS: I don't care what you say. You're late.	John shrugs off her harping
JOHN: I'm here now. I'm sorry I'm late. Now cool it.	

JESS: Rehearsal's been over forever. Where were you?	Beat 2 Jess lambastes John for being late
JOHN: Let's not start. How'd rehearsal go? Are you going to be good?	John pacifies Jess
JESS: Everyone is gone. They were picked up right after rehearsal. Everyone but me. And I don't like it when I'm here alone. This place echoes. Miss Terry said she'd stay but I told her to go on. She has children at home. And that boyfriend of hers. They'll be hungry. I told her I was used to it.	
JOHN: I'm here now. And I said I was sorry.	
JESS: Waiting, I mean. I'm used to waiting.	
JOHN: Get your stuff. Let's go. Mom'll be worried if we're not home soon.	
JESS: Forget it. I'm all right. *(Jessica drops the bomb.)*	
I called Mom; she'll pick me up on her way home.	Beat 3 Jess attacks John with the threat
JOHN: Call her back. Tell her I'm here.	John demands she call off their mother
JESS: It's okay. I've taken care of it. We're okay.	
JOHN: Give me your phone. Damn. Why'd you call her? Now she'll get on my case. And I don't need that. *(He goes to pick up Jessica's backpack.)*	
JESS: It was twenty minutes.	
JOHN: That's nothing.	
JESS: *(She snatches her bag from John.)* Get out of my bag. It's not nothing; it's twenty minutes. I was counting on you to pick me up and I didn't know if you'd ever come. Maybe I'd be stuck here all night! You are so self-absorbed.	Beat 4 Jess explodes John calms
JOHN: Call Mom. I'm here. I can take you home.	
JESS: I don't know why I thought you'd come anyway. I should know better. I'm almost a teenager. You've demonstrated that you're totally unreliable. That's what Mom says! You're never . . .	

JOHN: Cut it. Cut it right now. I'm here. It's okay.

JESS: It's not okay. IT'S NOT OKAY!

(Suddenly she is not so brave.) I'm alone in this big empty place. It's dark. It's late. I'm hungry. I waited for you . . . and you stood me up.	Beat 5 Jess pleads for understanding John defends himself

JOHN: There's a candy machine around front.

JESS: Look, just go on. Do . . . whatever. Just whatever you're doing. I'm fine.

JOHN: You're not crying, are you? *(Jess shakes her head.)* You didn't have to call Mom. She's on my case enough as it is. "Where were you? When will you? Why did you? How could you? You— you—you!" Me—me—me. I'm not a bad guy. I'm going on with my life. I've got to have my own space, some time by myself. My life! *(Pause.)*

She thinks I'm doing drugs.	**Unit 2: Barriers Fall—John admits there are problems with his behavior while Jessica confirms their mother's concerns**

JESS: Are you?

JOHN: Am I what?

JESS: Doing drugs?

JOHN: Jess, no! Jesus.

JESS: Well, I worry. So does Mom.

JOHN: Is that what Mom thinks? Does she talk with you about it?

JESS: Who else can she talk to? Look, I'm not a kid anymore. I read *Time* magazine. I watch *Dateline* . . .

JOHN: I'm not on drugs. I don't even drink.

JESS: You . . . OK, take off. I'll just wait for Mom.

(There is a moment of silence.)

JOHN: You and Mom talk about me?

JESS: What do you expect? Between work and school, she's got no time, no friends. So we talk. It's the least I can do. Listen to her, I mean. She says the girls at work are stuck up. And the other people in night school are so much younger than her. She thought this one teacher was cool, then he hit on her.

JOHN: What teacher? Who?

JESS: Like you're going to do something about it? Get off it. Anyway, it's nothing. Mom can take care of herself. That way, I mean. *(Pause.)* I wish she had some friends. It's tough for her, sure, but it's tough for me, too. I'd like her to be my mom again. You know. *(John nods.)*

JOHN: What does she say about me?

JESS: She worries. A lot. Sometimes you're late coming home and she doesn't know where you're at. And who you're with. And what you're doing. You know . . . she worries. She feels bad about having to work during the day and going to school at night. But she knows she has to get a better job so we'll have more money. She wishes there was someone who could help you . . . another guy. But there isn't.

JOHN: Look, Jess, I'm going to try and . . .

JESS: *(JESSICA phone rings in her book bag. She answers it.)* Hello. . . . Yeah, I'm still here. . . .

No, don't come. John's here now. He's going to take me home. . . . *(She glances at John, then turns away.)* He was talking to someone about a job. . . . He wanted to help out. But they're not hiring now. It's tough, you know. . . . Yeah, okay, I'll see you. *(She turns around and looks at her brother for a second.)*

JOHN: Thanks.

JESS: No problem. Let's go.

JOHN: Some of the guys and me were shooting hoops. Nothing else, just some running, talking, cutting fool. I lost track of the time.

JESS: You were having fun. That's important. But when I don't know where you are I worry. *(She realizes what she's said and how she's said it!)* Sometimes Mom's words just slip out of my

Unit 3: The Reconciliation— Jessica covers for John while John promises to be a better brother

mouth. Is that a good thing? Should that be happening? I don't want to be some precocious freak.

JOHN: You're not a freak. But you're right—you're too young to act like my mother. I really feel like an ass now.

JESS: *(Quoting something she's read.)* Guilt is not a productive emotion.

JOHN: Look, Jess, I don't know why I'm doing what I'm doing. I want to be a help to Mom and to you. I mean to. But when I'm home, I think about Dad and what happened and I start thinking . . . I just need to move. I just have to go. I'm not doing anything bad, not drugs or nothing. I wouldn't. I'm just . . . not doing much that helps I guess. I mean to. I'm going to.

JESS: Hurry up. I know you want to. We can't wait forever

(JESS starts to cross to pick up her tape player.

JOHN suddenly races to beat her to it.)

JOHN: Hold up. Just a minute. *(He starts rewinding the tape.)*

JOHN: Dance for me. Practice your dance.

JESS: John! Let's just go.

JOHN: Once. We've got time. Mom won't be home for a half-hour, at least. Just once.

JESS: I'll just fall again. I can't twirl without a partner.

JOHN: I'll be your partner. Trust me. We used to dance together . . . Right now.

JOHN starts the tape. At first reluctantly, then wholeheartedly, JESSICA practices her dance. At just the right moment, JOHN steps forward, holding up his hand for JESSICA to hold as she twirls. The music stops. SHE curtsies and JOHN bows to the empty house. JESSICA sees him and giggling, they grab her things and run off stage to the car and home.

END

Unit 4: The Reunion—John confirms his promise so Jessica accepts his goodwill

▥ CHARACTER

Dramatic action and character are intertwined almost beyond separation because the action of a modern realistic play is revealed entirely by what the characters say and do and by what is said about them by others. Character, then, is the instrument of the dramatic action; that is, all action happens through what characters do and say. The director must construct a detailed profile of each character in order to understand completely the people of the playscript. When armed with this knowledge, a director can effectively lead actors to fully realize their characters.

In real life, we say that character is the sum total of a person's behavior. But a play is not real life; it is highly selective and concentrated. In a playscript, characters are created by the playwright to move the action forward. They are a playwright's construct and as such are quite distilled. Their behavior is often quite limited in order to serve the specific needs of the plot. Understanding the difference between people in real life and people in plays is a first, important step in deciphering a playwright's characterization.

We understand characters in drama by noting what they do (action traits), what qualities they embody (personality traits), and how they operate in the world of the play (functional traits). These three aspects of characterization are collectively known as *character traits*.

Pivotal dramatic characters are also endowed by the playwrights with strong wants and needs that serve the plot. This aspect of characterization is called *superobjective,* a driving motive force that propels the character to action. The playwright may not always give a discernible superobjective to peripheral characters because they serve only a functional purpose in the world of the play. For example, a butler or waiter may have many identifiable character traits but no clear overriding superobjective.

A director's close examination of character traits and superobjectives will reveal much about how the playwright has characterized the people of the play.

Action Traits

Action traits illustrate character; they can reveal whether the character is abrupt, indecisive, or greedy, to name only a few qualities. Specific identifying action traits will emerge by studying the characters' conduct in the play. These include the choices characters embrace and act on, the decisions they come to that lead to action, and the behavior they exhibit. Action traits also can include the choices a character doesn't make, either knowingly or unknowingly, and the manner in which one character interacts with the other people of the play (see Figure 2.7).

Hedda Gabler, the title character in Ibsen's play, for example, fires one of her father's pistols at another character; she purposely destroys the only copy of a former friend's unpublished manuscript and then lies to her husband about why; she intentionally denigrates a new hat she knows belongs to her husband's beloved aunt; she gives the pistol fired earlier in the dramatic action to someone so that he might kill himself; she pretends she is showing a former suitor photographs of her honeymoon so that she might sit close to him; and she plays the piano just before she shoots her-

FIGURE 2.7   Action Traits. The things the playwright has his characters do in the course of the dramatic action are called action traits. This Sergeant in Neil Simon's *Biloxi Blues* is threatening to shoot a recruit with his service revolver. That trait helps define the kind of man he is. What about the seated soldier? Does he possess personality traits that warrent this treatment?

self in the play's final moments. These are only a few of the things Hedda does during the course of the play's action, but a profile of this title character is already quite boldly sketched just by noting her actions.

Characters can be enormously complex or rather transparent depending on the number of defining actions. In some plays (Greek tragedies, for example), even the central characters are defined by rather limited actions. Although their back-story may be complicated and their emotional range complex, their dramatized actions are quite few.

In modern plays, the author usually gives a central character dozens of defining actions. Yet, in long plays, peripheral characters are given few actions because they are at the edge of the plot. The central characters in a short play, on the other hand, because of the limited span of action, are delineated by relatively few actions.

No matter the number of behavioral actions a character engages in, these traits can illuminate the character's central defining qualities. The director should begin a character analysis by making a list of what each character in the play does. Action traits are central to delineating character.

Personality Traits

The qualities that make a character unique are called *personality traits,* which include temperament, abilities, background, appearance, and behavior. An analysis of the given circumstances will reveal much about the character's personality. It can provide the character's age, education, social class (rich, poor, struggling, upwardly mobile) and specific environment (kind of house or apartment, neat or messy). These givens can also suggest the character's general appearance (height, weight, attractiveness) and preferred clothing. The way the character speaks (or does not) discloses more specific traits (accent, vocabulary, locutions).

Personality traits not specifically indicated by the playwright can be fleshed out by the director through casting. If the given circumstances suggest the character is in her twenties but is not described in other ways and a slightly underweight twenty-six-year-old blond with short cropped hair is cast in the role, then this character also becomes a twenty-six-year-old lanky blond with short hair.

How a character relates to others and is perceived by others is also a significant aspect of personality. Is the character hot-headed? Reasonable? Friendly? Do other characters like her? Admire her? Despise her? Desire her? (See Figure 2.8.)

Values and ideological beliefs also define personality. What is "nearest and dearest" to the character? Is it money? Reputation? Appearances? Family? Moral rec-

FIGURE 2.8   Personality Traits. The character at the far right is mocking the woman with outstretched arms, one of her many personality traits, to create a comic moment in Shaw's *Heartbreak House.* Note also that the arrangement of characters on stage suggests that everyone is opposed to the character on the right.

titude? Identifying core beliefs and applying them to a written personality profile will result in a rather clear picture of the person this playwright has created.

The character's vocabulary and grammar are also insights to personality. Is the vocabulary dense? Polished? Is the syntax sophisticated? How does the character react to the vocabulary and grammar of others? The character's way of speaking can give much insight into personality. (See Figure 2.9.)

Functional Traits

Not only are characters given specific action and personality traits, but they also are made to serve a plot function. *Functional traits* help define how the character operates in the world of the play. The central character, the protagonist, is the one in conflict. The character that is pitted against the central character is the antagonist. Their dramatic functions are fairly clear. Stated in the boldest way, one is the hero, the other the villain.

Other, less important characters must be scrutinized to understand their structural role in the plot. One supporting character may serve as a contrast to the values

FIGURE 2.9   Body Language. This actress has translated Eliza Doolittle's personality traits into body language. In Bernard Shaw's *Pygmalion,* she moves from an underprivileged flower seller to a princess. What does posture say about her character traits at this moment in the dramatic action?

embodied by a major character. Another minor character may represent the choices the central character didn't explore. A third character, one with very little stage time, may serve to underscore the heartless way in which a son treats his father. Still another character may serve as the protagonist's confidante.

Analyzing functional traits in the television classic *I Love Lucy* may further clarify this concept. Almost without exception Lucy (Lucille Ball) is the protagonist. Her husband Desi (Desi Arnez) is often the antagonist. But many times an outsider served this function. Lucy's friend Ethel Mertz was almost always Lucy's confidante while Ethel's husband Fred was often Desi's confidante. In some episodes, Ethel was Lucy's foil—someone who thwarts another.

Discovering the character's dramatic function helps the director better appreciate the structure of the action. Understanding the functional traits also aids in the casting of characters. If a supporting character's function is to contrast with the protagonist, it may be useful to have actors with physical differences in height, coloring, voice, and so on. If that supporting character's function is to echo the protagonist, the opposite casting approach can be taken.

Superobjectives

Because characters in plays are a distillation of qualities, each major character is driven by one overriding want or need, called the *superobjective*. This driving force accounts for each of the character's action traits. The superobjective, then, is a global statement that represents the person's totality in the world of the play's action.

The superobjective of the major characters must collide so that conflict is possible. If the protagonist's superobjective is *to keep my family safely together,* then the antagonist's superobjective may be *to insinuate myself into that family unit.* Whatever the superobjective, it must account for the character's action traits. Figure 2.10 describes some character traits and superobjectives.

There are other superobjective characteristics. Constantin Stanislavski, the great Russian acting teacher and director, believed a superobjective should do the following:

- Encompass all of the character's individual objectives
- Be directed toward other characters and not inward
- Reflect the inner life of the character rather than the character's outward, physical life
- Relate to the play's larger issue
- Be stated as a "to" construction followed by an active verb ("to find a place where I can rest")

Minor characters, because they are at the edges of the action, may not have a readily identified superobjective that is based on action and personality traits. Some characters seem to be motivated solely by their functional traits. The director can help the actors who play these parts by devising a superobjective that is in keeping with their function and is consistent with their other traits.

FIGURE 2.10 Character Traits and Superobjectives. A character can have many action and personality traits but only one superobjective and functional trait.

Action Traits *There Can Be Many*	Personality Traits *There Can Be Many*	Functional Traits *Always Only One*	Superobjectives *Always Only One*
■ Breaks someone's arm ■ Packs boxes to move out ■ Sells the family home ■ Does card tricks ■ Steals private papers ■ Refuses to give spouse medicine	■ Speaks in an Ozark's dialect ■ Described as "terribly attractive" ■ Dresses like a "dandy" ■ Easily startled ■ Confident ■ Sexy ■ Appears shy ■ Has thinning hair	■ Protagonist ("hero") ■ Antagonist ("villain") ■ Confidante ■ Foil ■ Representative of the community ■ Contrasts with another character's traits	■ To provide for family ■ To hide the truth about father ■ To avenge father's death ■ To preserve the marriage ■ To discover the truth ■ To find security

The Actor and the Character

Character development is a partnership between the playwright and the actor. The actor enriches, develops, and enhances what the playwright sketches out. A specific character in a specific play can seem quite different to an audience when enacted by two unique actresses even though they are saying the same playwright's words. Casting, then, becomes an important tool for shaping character (see Figure 2.11).

Janet McTeer earned great acclaim in 1997 as Nora in Ibsen's *A Doll's House,* prompting critics in England and the United States to exclaim that they never really knew that Ibsen's feminist tract could be as riveting as it was in the production directed by Anthony Page.

TIP: Interpretation

Phrasing a superobjective is an important act of directorial interpretation. Two directors, working on the same playscript, may devise quite different superobjectives for the same character; both may be valid and supported by the text. Because each director brings different experiences, different ways to looking at the world, and different approaches to reality to this hypothetical script, their interpretations and its major characters are bound to diverge. That is, one superobjective is not "wrong" and the other one is not necessarily "right." Both may be valid in the context of the production each director is planning.

FIGURE 2.11   The Character Emerges. The character of Libby Price here speaks directly to the audience as a narrator, setting out part of the back-story, in Thomas Gibbons' *Bee-Luther-Hatchie*. These moments of direct address are a part of Libby's functional traits as set forth by the author. But why is Libby dressed in trousers, hat, suspenders? Who made the choice that she should appear as a man— actor? director? collaboration?

Nora is usually cast as a diminutive person and played with some reserve. She is often seen as a meek, shy woman. Ms. McTeer is tall, a bit over six feet, and described by one observer as "strapping." She played Nora first as a caged, squirrel-like flibbertigibbet. She gave a quite surprisingly hyperrendition of the opening act. However, by the final confrontation scene between husband and wife, when Nora makes the decision to leave her family to find herself, the decision appears to surprise Nora as much as her husband.

The idea for this production, which won Olivier Awards in England and Tony Awards in New York, came from the actress herself. She believed past productions had portrayed Nora in a dull marriage, already dead when the curtain rises. The key to making the play work was casting a virile, young husband to project a sexually active marriage. This casting allowed Nora more freedom to grow. The result was an unforgettable *A Doll's House,* one that presented a startling new Nora. Clearly Janet McTeer was a collaborator with Ibsen in creating a newly minted character.

The director must consider what the actors themselves bring to the roles they will play. These actor traits include their personal qualities (height, weight, coloring, and gender) as well as their individual demeanor.

Experiences

Character Traits

Return again to the script you divided into beginning, middle, and end. Now identify the action, personality, and functional traits of each character. Share your analysis with the group.

Superobjectives

Identify the superobjective of each character in this same play. Share your analysis with the group. Be prepared to explain your choices.

▚▚▚ MEANING

Plot is often about what happens next; *meaning* is the significance of those events in a wider context. If the stage director perceives no larger meaning, then the audience's enjoyment of a production is limited to discovering only what happens next.

Sometimes moment-by-moment dramatized incidents without a core meaning may be acceptable to audiences. Television soap operas, for instance, seldom are concerned with larger meanings. They exist in an intellectual vacuum to present a set of characters in conflict. The audience is expected to be interested (and often is) only in what happens next to the characters who are caught up in incest, infidelity, scandal, knavery, and illicit romance.

In the theatre, most playscripts reward the audience by presenting compelling incidents *and* a meaning that resonates throughout the theatrical experience. The vitality of a play's core meaning, its universality, gives significance to a playscript that is broader than its specific events and characters.

Sometimes this aspect of a play is called theme, moral, or message. No matter what it is called, important plays have a core, which gives them resonance beyond their plot and characters. It is imperative that the director try to uncover and understand the core meaning in order to enhance it during the directorial process.

Can a playscript embody more than one core meaning? The answer lies in the individual playscript. Is it rich with meaning, or is it a thin bedroom farce? The more ambitious the author and the more successful the playscript, the more room there is to find multiple meanings. A production of David Rabe's *Streamers* might emphasize "the nature of fear that cripples"; another production might emphasize another quite different meaning. An extended example may help clarify this seeming paradox.

Action and Meaning

Consider the events of *The Emperor's New Clothes.* In this fable, a swindler convinces the Emperor that he has sewn a suit of clothes so ethereal and perfect that only the most noble of people can see it. The Emperor cannot admit that there are no clothes at all, so he parades through his kingdom in the nude. All of his subjects are conned into believing the lie and, so as not to admit to being less than noble, no one admits that the Emperor is naked. Instead, they all praise the beauty of the Emperor's raiment. Only a child speaks the truth: "The Emperor is naked."

Do these events have meaning? If so, what meaning? In truth, there could be many meanings, including the following:

- All people want to appear better than they are, even when they must defy common sense.
- People are afraid to say what they think when it differs from what others believe.
- People in power are insecure because they are only human.
- People believe what they are told.
- There's a sucker born every minute—and even an important leader is not safe from swindlers.
- Only children are honest.

One might even imagine a meaning that pronounces that the most beautiful thing of all is the human body. There could be other core meanings as well.

Now imagine a play based on *The Emperor's New Clothes.* The action units could be arranged to dramatize any of the core meanings just listed. How might current events—in politics, perhaps—lead an audience to choose some of these meanings to emphasize over others? How might a director's concept emphasize different aspects of the play to underscore the meaning in one particular production?

Finding and Phrasing a Core Meaning

Well-regarded plays are open to many valid core interpretations. It is often said that one aspect of a play's greatness is the variety of interpretations it can embrace. Finding a supportable meaning in plays, such as *Hamlet, Macbeth,* or *Romeo and Juliet,* can be one of the director's most important interpretive acts. These plays are so rich in character and action that they will support several core meanings, depending on the director's emphasis of certain aspects of the production and the deemphasis of other aspects.

There are many clues to help the director uncover a play's meaning. The director might undertake a closer look at the play's title for guidance, examine key speeches within the play, or evaluate the qualities of the play's major character. Sometimes research into the playwright's background and other playscripts is helpful.

Titles

The play's title is a starting point. An examination of the playscript's action in relationship to the title may reveal the play's core meaning(s) and lead the director to a

TIP: Avoid Confusion

A core meaning should not be confused with what happens to the central character. Note that in the example of *The Emperor's New Clothes* none of the possible core meanings offered included the main character's realization: "I'm naked!" or " I've been cheated!"

A playscript's core meaning is greater than the conflict and realization of the main character. The core meaning of plays ideally should connect to the characters' realizations, but the core meaning is not the realization.

In *The Glass Menagerie,* Tom discovers that he must abandon his home, mother, and sister if he is to survive as an artist. One core meaning for *The Glass Menagerie* might be stated this way:

Modern urban and industrial society leaves no safe space for the fragile and emotionally needy to live.

This is only one possible core meaning; *Menagerie* is a great play that can support multiple interpretations. Note there is no mention of the characters of Tom, Amanda, Laura, or Jim in this core meaning.

In *Oedipus Rex,* the central character discovers that he has killed his father and married his mother. One core meaning of this play might be expressed this way:

People who let their pride in themselves blind them to reality are fated for tragedy.

Again, here there is no mention of Oedipus or Jocasta.

---

playable interpretation. Does the title suggest a larger context? How does the action relate to the title? Consider enigmatic titles such as *Long Day's Journey into Night, A Streetcar Named Desire,* or *The Little Foxes.* Might the key to unlocking the meaning's core be found in titles as rich as these?

Willy Loman, the salesman in *Death of a Salesman,* explains the meaning of the play's title in an extended speech in the second act. He believes that salesmen die in luxury wearing "green velvet slippers" and are missed, respected, and mourned by hundreds of colleagues. Selling, Willy asserts, is a noble profession. The director may take this speech in the middle of the play to stand for Willy's value system, which will lead directly to his death. Together with material found in other key speeches and information about Willy, the director can formulate a core meaning.

Key Speeches
There may be important speeches within the playscript that will unlock the core. Does a character philosophize? If so, about what? Might this speech hold a clue to the playscript's larger meaning? Key speeches need not be said by the protagonist in order to lead the director to a supportable core meaning.

In the Epilogue of Miller's *Death of a Salesman,* Charley says of Willy Loman, the salesman who has just killed himself: "Nobody dast blame this man." The use of the strange word *dast* for *dare not* alerts us to pay attention to what Charley has to say. He notes that Willy was a salesman, and that for a salesman, "there is no rock bottom to the life." Willy is, like all salesmen, Charley says, is "a man way out there in the blue, riding on a smile and a shoeshine." And when people don't smile back, "that's an earthquake."

Charley, whose character's function is to mirror the path Willy has not taken in his job choice, in his values, and in his parenting, sums up Willy's life by saying; "A salesman is got to dream, boy. It comes with the territory." Charley is telling us that Willy had a value system even though it was misguided because it depended on being well liked, rather than being based on sterner moral fiber.

For some directors, this speech is the key to unlocking the core meaning of *Death of a Salesman.*

The Central Character

The personality and action traits of the central character can prompt the director to understand the play's core meaning. Again, in *Death of a Salesman,* we note Willy's surname, Loman. He is a *low* man—a common man, an ordinary man—and as such stands for all citizens in post World War II America. He is also a man of the earth, a *loam* man.

Several times during the play Willy insists that it is not only important to be "liked" but to be "well liked." He values the daring of his sons as he encourages them to steal building materials from a nearby construction site. Willy demeans the academic success of his neighbor's child in favor of the adoration his eldest son garners as a football hero. Throughout the play, he wonders if he is teaching the right values to his sons. Armed with this information, and other evidence, the director can deduce a compelling core meaning.

Phrasing a Core Meaning

A play's core meaning should be distilled to a phrase or, at the most, a sentence or two. The director might say telegraphically that a play is "about fear." A fuller phrasing of the core becomes: "The way we respond to fear defines in unpredictable ways who we are." Or, "Fear can ruin us." Note that this phrasing emphasizes the broader meaning of the playscript; it does not reflect what specifically happens to the main characters.

A core meaning for *Oedipus Rex,* which states "Oedipus learns that he should not try to circumvent the Gods," takes a somewhat narrow view of this great play. A more useful statement should focus on the larger meaning(s) bound up in *Oedipus Rex.*

A taut, universal phrasing will focus the director's attention on a play's core meaning. This terse statement doesn't imply that the playscript is diminished or reduced in stature to a short phrase or a simple sentence. It, instead, pinpoints the playscript's core meaning that the director will develop during production.

Requirements of a Core Statement

Once the core statement is constructed, the director should test it by asking some direct questions:

- Does the core statement accommodate the central action?
- Can the major characters be better understood in light of the core statement?
- Does the core statement reflect the given circumstances?

TIP: What a Title Can Reveal

Titles can offer specific insight to the interpreter of a playscript, especially the director and designers. More metaphoric, evocative titles, while not very specific, still can guide the interpreter.

Cat on a Hot Tin Roof, a colorful Southern locution, communicates the hothouse, restless atmosphere of this Tennessee Williams play. It draws attention to the character of Maggie who is described in the dialogue as behaving like a cat on a hot tin roof.

Arthur Miller's *Death of a Salesman* tells the audience the main character's fate before they enter the theatre. Referring to the protagonist, Willy Loman, by an impersonal job description, echoes society's callousness to the working man, one of Miller's themes.

Sometimes the title will require research to reveal all of its potency. Lorraine Hansberry's *A Raisin in the Sun* has a beautiful title: rich, evocative, open-ended. It enriches our understanding of Hansberry's drama to know that the title is a quote from a famous poem by Langston Hughes.

With this poem in mind, one's attention is drawn to the theme of the characters' dreams, meaning in this instance, their ambitions. More important, the characters' flaws are seen as the result of the thwarting of their ambitions—the deferral of their dreams—rendering their fates tragic, not just melodramatic.

If the answer to these questions is positive, the director knows the core statement will lead to an effective, balanced production.

As noted in *The Emperor's New Clothes* example, a story can have several valid core meanings. Constructing the best core statement for a specific production of a playscript is part analysis and part artistry. It must be supported by the playwright's words, but the core statement also needs to embrace other considerations, which could include currents events, the artists involved in the production, or factors outside the world of the play.

Current Political or Social Events

Sophocles' *Antigone* from the fifth century BC, for example, in the twentieth century became an important play for expressing the opposition between private conscience and public duty. In the playscript, a disastrous civil war leaves the leaders of both sides, two brother princes, dead. The new ruler prevents the burial of one brother whom he declares a traitor. Their sister, the Princess Antigone, defies the new ruler and buries her brother even though it means the punishment of death. She is motivated by the strength of her religious beliefs in the importance of burial.

A recent production of *Antigone* sets the play in the present day in an imaginary Middle Eastern kingdom. The chorus part was divided among three choruses: local religious leaders, local military leaders, and a group of the international press. Television monitors showed events not dramatized in the original play. Motivated by the ruinous battles in Afghanistan and the endless fighting between Palestinians and Israelis, the director chose this approach as a way of reshaping the play's issues without altering the script. His core statement seemed to be: "What price will we pay, can we pay, must we pay in exchange for order? Not every prisoner of conscience is a heroine or hero." The U.S. seems to be facing a similar crisis in light of encroaching terrorism as well as the instability in Iraq.

Recently, a fresh stage adaptation of Ovid's *Metamorphoses* opened in a small, not-for-profit Off-Broadway theatre. The play retells stories from Greek myth, many of which involve love triumphing over death or love lasting past death. The production has a gimmick of a sort: The main scenery is a large pool of water in which the actors move, float, fight, and so on. The play met with a stronger audience response in New York than it had received elsewhere and soon moved to a Broadway house for an open-ended commercial run.

Critics remarked on how meaningful the stories are because the play happened to open within a few months of the World Trade Center attack. New Yorkers—perhaps all Americans—are now sensitive to stories of love and loss. The play's use of myth allowed the audience a sense of distance from which to relive and absorb their losses, one of the highest effects of art. The director did not develop her concept in response to recent crises, but nevertheless the impact of the production's existing core statement happened to be underscored by those events.

Personalities of the Actors and Designers

Frequently in commercial theatres, as well as not-for-profit venues, a star actor can, justifiably, influence the direction a production takes. The Actor and the Character section earlier in this chapter describes how British actor Janet McTeer reshaped the core interpretation of *A Doll's House.*

Designers can be influential too. Stephen Daldry's startling interpretation of *An Inspector Calls,* described in the Prologue of this book, was greatly influenced by Ian MacNeil's striking hydraulic design, which allowed the miniature house to open, crumble, and reerect itself.

Other Influences

The nature of the producing circumstances can often shape the director's approach to a production. If the playing space is a storefront in Selma, Alabama, then a production of *Romeo and Juliet* may be driven by the racial tensions that once erupted in that town. Instead of warring Italian families, the Shakespeare tragedy could become an interracial struggle motivated by prejudice.

Sometimes just the human need for variety, whimsy, and delight can drive the director to concoct a surprising core statement. For the purposes of this investigation into the art and craft of directing, the beginning director is urged to put whimsy aside and deal with a clear and straightforward core statement.

Use the Core Statement

The *core statement* is the map for the production, the master recipe that will guide what ingredients are used and how they will be combined. Armed with a concise core statement, a director can make many interpretative decisions, including those of casting, setting, and lighting, to bring emphasis to the play's stated meaning. Whenever choices occur, the director measures the outcomes of those choices against the playscript's core.

Experiences

Core Meaning

Using the short play you will direct for your first project, determine a core statement for your production. It should be a brief statement that meets the requirements for a core statement listed before. Turn in the core statement to your instructor for a response.

Think back to a recent play or musical you saw in a theatre and phrase a core meaning that seemed to drive the production. Share your perceptions with the group.

▬ KEY TERMS

With sufficient study of Step Two, you should be able to fully define the following terms:

- Action traits
- Action unit
- Antagonist
- Beat
- Climax
- Core meaning
- Falling action
- French scene
- Functional traits
- Given circumstances
- Inciting incident
- Objective
- Personality traits
- Plot
- Protagonist
- Rising action
- Scene
- Story
- Superobjective
- Verbs

■■■■ WEB CONNECTIONS FOR MORE . . .

These Web sites will help you understand more about Analyzing and Researching the Playscript.

- A number of playwrights were mentioned in this step. If you want to know more about them, use a search engine like Google and enter one name at a time; you will be pointed to a variety of sites. Have fun searching the Web and learning more about these important authors: Paula Vogel, Samuel Beckett, Arthur Miller, Lorraine Hansberry, Tennessee Williams, Henrik Ibsen, Eugene O'Neill, Lillian Hellman, Sophocles, and any others you may want to research.
- Use the URL *www.theatrehistory.com/american* to look up other directors or playwrights. This site is somewhat limited but significant information can be found there.
- Using a search engine like Google, find reviews of recent movies and plays to see if the reviewer came to grips with the core meaning.

S T E P

3

Conceiving the Production

Once the playscript is selected and analyzed, the director must then imagine the production for a specific actor–audience relationship in a specific theatre. Performance spaces come in many sizes and shapes, but the director is obligated to make the production effective in the one that will be used, even if that theatre space seems less than ideal. The director rarely has the luxury of selecting the actor–audience relationship that is best suited to the playscript to be staged. However rare this opportunity may be, the beginning director is advised to consider how the actor–audience relationship at hand can be used to the production's best advantage.

▮▮ STAGE CONFIGURATIONS

Four architectural configurations have emerged from the theatre's long history. These actor–audience relationships encompass the well-known proscenium stage and its antithesis, the arena stage. The thrust and alley stages can be seen as variations of the proscenium and arena configurations. The twentieth century has added the idea of performing in found space, which can mimic one of these four configurations, combine them, or invent new ones. An examination of each configuration will reveal characteristics that distinguish each actor–audience relationship.

The Proscenium Stage

The most familiar actor–audience relationship is the *proscenium* theatre, or picture-frame stage. Here the picture frame, called the *proscenium arch,* separates the actors from the audience by having them face one another (see Figure 3.1). Even if there is not an elaborate architectural picture frame, this separation of actor and audience is a well-established theatrical custom known as the *fourth-wall* convention. This convention imagines that one wall of a room is missing and that the audience is eavesdropping while the actors are unaware of their presence.

In this century, the fourth-wall convention is much honored in the breach because playwrights have characters speak directly to the audience, enter and exit from the auditorium, and in other ways have characters behave as if they are aware of the

FIGURE 3.1 The Proscenium Stage. This schematic plan also shows the relative position of the orchestra pit, which is used for musicals and operas.

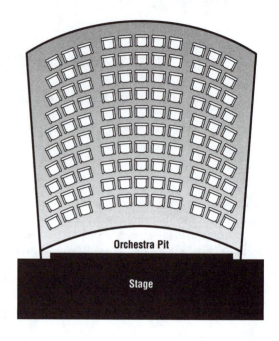

audience. Contemporary directors have devised productions of plays written for the fourth-wall spaces that gain import and meaning by shattering the conventions of the traditional space, thwarting the illusionistic expectation of the audience.

Proscenium theatres became the dominant theatrical space by the end of the seventeenth century. Opera houses, ballet venues, and the majority of Broadway theatres use the picture-frame stage. Proscenium theatres can house startling scenic effects, change settings efficiently, and present the most lifelike depictions of reality because the setting is seen by the audience from only one side.

Proscenium spaces can be quite intimate, designed to hold fewer than two hundred spectators, as many Off-Broadway theatres do, or they can be as vast as Radio City Music Hall in New York, seating six thousand spectators.

The Arena Stage

In this configuration, the audience surrounds the playing space on all sides. It is the antithesis of the proscenium stage. Theatre-in-the-round spaces, as *arena* stages are sometimes called, can be quite intimate because spectators "wrap around" the players (see Figure 3.2). Actors enter from aisles or from tunnels running underneath banks of seats. Arena configurations can be either a square with the audience seated behind each side of the stage, or circular with the audience arcing around the playing space. Scenic elements are minimal because large set pieces would obstruct the audience's view. For that reason, designs for most arena stages use half-walls, furniture,

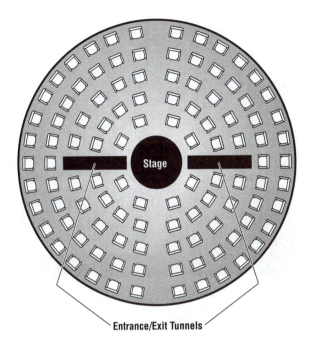

FIGURE 3.2   The Arena Stage. In the arena configuration, the audience surrounds the players.

and floor coverings to depict interior locales. The aptly named Arena Stage in Washington, DC, is the best known of the many arena stages in the United States.

The Thrust Stage

The audience surrounds the playing space on three sides in a *thrust* space (see Figure 3.3). The fourth side is often a neutral, architectural wall. Some thrust stages are designed to have a flexible back wall, which may be curtained to suggest neutrality or contain scenic elements that reflect the given circumstances of a specific playscript. Entrances and exits are made through the audience, from under the audience through tunnel-like openings, and from the back wall.

The playing area juts into the audience and is often raised to separate the actors from the audience. While furniture and low set pieces are welcomed in this space, detailed scenery is confined to the one back wall. Like the arena, the audience is closer to the players than they would be in a proscenium arrangement seating the same number of patrons.

Thrust stages are quite popular now in America's regional, nonprofit theatres. Many of the Western world's great plays were written specifically for this actor–audience arrangement. These plays include those from ancient Greece, the comedies of Plautus from Roman times, the improvised comedies of the Italian *commedia del'arte,* and those of Shakespeare and his many contemporaries. The Festival Theatre in Stratford, Canada, and the Guthrie Theatre in Minneapolis are two world-renowned thrust theaters, as is the Mark Taper Forum in Los Angeles.

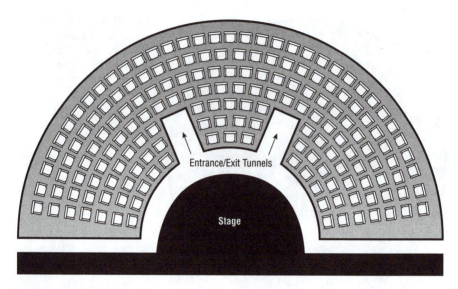

FIGURE 3.3   The Thrust Stage. The back wall of this stage can accommodate an architectural façade or scenic elements.

The Alley Stage

In this arrangement, the audience sits on two sides of a playing space that is longer than it is wide. The actors occupy the *alley* between the audience. Like the arena and thrust configurations, scenic enhancement is minimal. It is possible, however, to place quite detailed scenic elements at either end of the alley.

Some theatres can be configured in any of these four arrangements. One of the most flexible stages in New York City is housed in the Circle In The Square theatre in midtown Manhattan. This space has seen plays staged in arena, thrust, and alley arrangements. Most often, the audience is shaped like a giant U at the top of which is the concealing wall. Sometimes when seating is placed at the top of the U, the space becomes an arena theatre. At other times, when seating is removed from the bottom of the U, players can enter and exit from a tunnel situated under the audience, turning the actor–audience relationship into an alley stage.

Found Stages

This kind of stage houses performances in existing structures that were not originally designed to be theatres. Here the director and the designers fashion an actor–audience relationship that fits the play and, most important, the found space, which could resemble proscenium, arena, thrust, or alley configurations. They can also be shaped as an L, an X, or a Y, or any other practical configuration. Found spaces could be a street corner, the lobby of a building, a stairway, or a hallway.

TIP: Begin with a Proscenium Space

Much is made of the differences between the proscenium stage and other actor–audience configurations. In truth, for directors, the technical differences are smaller than many commentators suggest.

In any space, the director must choose the playscript, analyze it, cast it, work with designers and actors, and so on. The main differences are in devising a ground plan and blocking the action. Even here, the differences are not extreme.

For the ground plan, the director must ask the same questions in all environments: Are there enough acting areas? Are specific plot requirements met? Can I mo-

tivate actors to use all of the stage area? Can the playscript's climax be effectively staged? Similarly, in blocking the director is still interested in focus, variety, tempo, picturization, and the like. Although this text focuses on proscenium staging, the student can apply these guidelines to any actor–audience configuration.

In a more practical vein, the space you use to stage productions for this course most likely will be a classroom setup like a proscenium space. If the class is fortunate enough to have a flexible black-box performance space, I still strongly recommend beginning with proscenium staging.

Some Off-Broadway and Off-Off Broadway theatres are fashioned in found spaces and do not strictly conform to the four actor–audience relationships just described. If directors are knowledgeable about proscenium, thrust, arena, and alley spaces, they can easily adapt their techniques to a found space.

■ OVERVIEW

Step Three is devoted to the process of conceiving a production for a specific space. The step includes information about formulating a concept that will guide the production through rehearsals, discovering the aural possibilities in the playscript, as well as devising a ground plan. Step Three, then is given over to helping the audience to see and to hear the playscript. A prompt book will aid the director in organizing the production during rehearsals and performance.

The Prompt Book

When fully completed, a *prompt book* is like a conductor's score for a symphony performance. It contains all of the composer's music as well as the conductor's interpretive notations that will be used to guide the conductor during a performance. A theatrical prompt book is the director's plan for the production. It contains the director's research, interpretations, and plans for the production; in fact, it can contain anything the director believes is important to the production's conception, rehearsal, and performance.

The heart of a prompt (a term that reflects its first use—to nudge the actor's memory) book is an especially prepared copy of the playscript, which is a mandatory tool for the director and stage manager. In addition to a fully notated script, the prompt book is a repository for all kinds of background materials, including:

- The playwright's background, including a description of the theatre of his time
- Notes on the play's structure
- Character analysis
- World of the play, including concept statement
- Aural notes
- Ground plan
- French scene analysis
- Planning calendar
- Rehearsal schedule
- Contact sheet
- Director's rehearsal journal
- Reviews

When the production is over, the prompt book is the production's historical record.

A fully notated prompt book becomes the blueprint of the performance for the stage manager; it is from this book that she "calls the show"—tells the lighting and sound operators when they should move into the next cue. The stage manager runs the production beginning with technical rehearsals through to all performances. The stage manager notes all set, light, and sound cues in the prompt book. There should also be a contact sheet for all personnel connected with the performance, including home and work telephone numbers and email addresses, so that they can be reached easily and quickly.

A prompt book represents the director's research and becomes a paper record of the production. If the director preblocks the production, then those notations are in-

---

TIP: Prompt Book Mechanics

1. Use a three-ring notebook with heavy weight filler paper, which will withstand constant use and erasures.
2. Attach a page of script to the right-hand page and leave the left page blank. The director uses the blank page for notes on blocking and other staging ideas.
3. Use a pencil with a functioning eraser for notations. Expect to erase.
4. The director could use tab dividers to separate research and background mate-rials from the script. There could be a tab for sections on the playwright (if necessary), production concept, required properties, notes on setting and ground plan, aural enhancements, planning calendar, script analysis, and character analysis/descriptions. Tabs could be used for scene-by-scene divisions too.

cluded in the prompt script. The director should use the prompt book at every rehearsal, noting new blocking, revising predetermined blocking, making notes about props that have been added, and any other useful information.

■ GOALS

When you have studied Step Three, you should be able to do the following:

■ Prepare a useful prompt book
■ Phrase a production metaphor
■ Examine the playscript to determine its emotional, visual, and aural worlds
■ Devise a concept that will guide the production through rehearsals
■ Explore the sonic possibilities in a playscript
■ Explain the importance of a workable ground plan
■ Devise a functional ground plan for a specific production
■ Test a ground plan for effectiveness

■ THE WORLD OF THE PLAY

If you have studied Step Two with care, and applied those principles to the playscript you will direct, you should understand that play quite well. You have discovered the playscript's structure, divided it into units and beats, unearthed its larger meaning, and examined the characters to understand how they function as personalities and as agents of the dramatic action.

The next step is to imagine the play whole again, reinforced by the knowledge gained through analysis. Read it once more to organize your global impression of the entire script. During this reading, you should try to let the pattern of the whole play emerge. Try to enter the imaginary world of the playscript as you conjure it.

Even playscripts we consider to be realistic—that is, plays that correspond to our sense of the day-to-day world—create their own unique worlds. Pearl Cleage's *Blues for an Alabama Sky* and Lorraine Hansberry's *A Raisin in the Sun* have much in common. For instance, both plays are by African American women, both deal exclusively with the experiences of African American characters, both plays have characters with a similar motive (to make a better life for themselves), both take place in large cities (Chicago and New York), yet the plays have quite distinct and individual worlds. One depicts the waning excitement of the Harlem Renaissance just after the 1929 stock market crash. The other depicts late 1950s Chicago tenement life where three generations of a family share the same crowded apartment.

Cleage and Hansberry, like other playwrights, cannot show everything about the characters they set into action. To make an emotional impact, what is shown is often heightened and compressed. Another playwright could take the same characters and the same situations that captivated Cleage and Hansberry and construct very different plays by making different choices. A playwright's choice of what to show and how to show it creates a playscript's unique world.

Imagination

The director must fully understand the playscript's world—emotionally, intellectually, and intuitively—in order to recreate that world on the stage (see Figure 3.4). The beginning director may be forced to examine the play in ways that may seem unconventional. Apart from the plot, how does one play differ from another? How does one picture in an art museum differ from another? The answer lies in how we perceive a play or a portrait.

Imagine taking a color picture of yourself with an instant camera. Now imagine that a couple self-portraits painted by great artists are set beside that photo. Although each image is a likeness of a recognizable person, the photo you take and the paintings will be very different and will give different emotional effects.

If one of the paintings is a self-portrait by, say, Van Gogh, you surely will notice the brush strokes, which are rhythmic, often curving into whirls. The colors are exaggerated with great contrasts next to each other—green next to red, blue next to yellow. The background is bright and flat. The face is still but the painting expresses great motion, even great emotion or turmoil.

FIGURE 3.4 The Design Team.
(a) As the leader of the design team, the director (*center*) is responsible for the visual appearance of the production including the sets, costumes, props, makeup, scene changes, and lights. Here he collaborates with the assistant set designer (who prepared the model seen in (b)), technical director, production designer, lighting designer (*slightly behind the director*), and the set designer. The costume designer is not pictured. Beginning directors, of course, will not have a design team like this to help with the first directing experiences; they will do it all themselves. However, the function of these designers must be understood if the director is to develop as an artist and a craftsperson.

Imagine that one of the self-portraits is by Rembrandt. The colors are restrained, largely earth tones of red, tan, brown, and black. The lighting is subdued and the edges of the painting recede into darkness. Rembrandt looks out of the canvas at rest, seeming confident and masterful, although there is the hint of a hidden private life beneath the calm surface.

Finally, consider the snapshot of yourself. The colors are a little exaggerated perhaps. If you used a flash, you look brighter and flatter than you normally do. Your expression is trapped but still captures one of your many moods. You may even say, "Oh, this picture doesn't look like me," but your friends may disagree and say, "Yes, it *does!*"

Even artworks that are more or less realistic, such as in the case of the three imagined self-portraits, create a unique world. The differences between the worlds created in individual paintings (and in individual plays) are usually the most interesting part of the art. They reflect the personality of the artist and lead a viewer to see the day-to-day world in new ways.

Many playscripts have worlds that correspond, it seems, to the photo: They reflect very much the day-to-day world we think we live in or they resemble the world of many other plays being written today. Yet other scripts have worlds that are strikingly different and unexpected. Some playwrights have a signature world that is unique to their writings. If you know several plays by Harold Pinter, you will be able to describe his singular approach to reality. The same could be said for Shakespeare's comedies. But even though the world of *As You Like It* may have many similarities to the world of *Twelfth Night,* they are quite different constructs.

Presentational and Representational Approaches

One of the most significant questions a director must ask is: "Where are we?" To what extent will this production be presentational? Representational? Is the audience in a theatrical space, that is, a theatre? Or is the stage to give the illusion of a specific place at a specific time? The implications of these questions are important for both the director and the designers (see Figures 3.5 and 3.6).

Presentational productions are highly *theatrical; that is, they readily admit that they take place in a theatre.* Representational productions try to give the illusion that they take place in a locale that is not a theatre (e.g., in a living room or bar or attic).

Some playscripts seem very much at home reveling in the exterior trappings of reality—walls, doors, furniture, windows—while others seem to celebrate the neutral acting platform with several entrances and exits that allow the characters to come and go quickly and without the gear associated with realistic illusion. It is the difference between the perceived needs of *Romeo and Juliet* or *Macbeth* as opposed to those of *A Doll's House* or *Hedda Gabler.* The way in which these hypothetical productions might be staged will depend on the demands of the script, the performance space, the director's concept, and the theatre conventions prevalent at the moment.

For example, in late nineteenth-century London, it was customary to stage *Romeo and Juliet* as illusionistically as possible with painted drops, wings, and set

FIGURE 3.5   Visual Imagination. The director and the designer agreed on an abstract approach to the visual world for this production of *As You Like It.* The permanent setting is a metal jungle gym surrounded by screens of transparent material that could be raised or lowered to accommodate the several locations cited in the script. The screen panels take light easily and thus reflect both the *light* and *dark* atmospheres embodied in Shakespeare's script. The designer in Figure 3.4 imagined what the famous letter scene in the Forest of Arden might look like. The moon in the background is made of strips of acrylic, which accepts light and seems to glow.

pieces that depicted specific locations mentioned in the text. In this century, the directorial strategy for Shakespeare's plays is a very theatrical approach to the text that denies illusionism. Throughout most of the twentieth century, it was usual to stage *A Doll's House* and *Hedda Gabler* using the fourth-wall convention of the proscenium. Now one sees productions of representational scripts, such as these two Ibsen classics, performed eclectically in whatever space is available.

If creatively directed and designed, any playing space—whether arena, alley, thrust, or proscenium—can successfully house a presentational or representational production. Baz Luhrmann's Broadway production of the nineteenth-century opera *La Boheme* is performed in an 1,800-seat proscenium theatre, but his production thrives on the collision between the representational and the presentational. There is always representational scenery on stage but at the same time, at the edge of the sets, the audience sees the stagehands manipulating the illusionistic effects.

FIGURE 3.6 Director and Designer Collaborate. This is the designer's conception of what the *As You Like It* concluding wedding scene might look like. Compare this drawing to the photograph (see Figure 3.7) of the actual staging of that scene. How closely did the director follow the designer's suggestions? How closely does the actual set follow the designer's imagination?

For example, in an attic loft, a fireplace gives off light that plays on the faces of some of the actors. The walls of the garret receive the ripples of firelight too. But also visible to the audience are the stagehands operating the modern lighting instruments to produce the firelight. Further, scene changes take place in full view of the audience. Luhrmann's costly production could have hidden the source of the lighting or the set changes; however, the director and his designer wanted to exploit the tension between presentational and representational approaches.

Metaphor

Because playwrights create new worlds every time they write, we have little shared language to describe those worlds. A telling metaphor can help pinpoint, and thus communicate, to the production team and actors, the director's distilled response to the visual images of the playscript.

A *metaphor* is a term or phrase that compares two quite dissimilar things in order to suggest an unlikely comparison. A metaphor, while rich in association, is not a literal correlation of the things compared. Shakespeare's phrase, "All the world's a stage . . . ," is a quite famous metaphor that draws a relationship between life and theatre. This analogy is richly suggestive but not literal. Some suggestions of Shakespeare's metaphor include "In real life, people play roles when required," or "Dramatic events happen everywhere," and so on.

A metaphor can translate a play's action into an evocative context. The metaphor is not the play but a way of allowing an audience to see and hear the play. The director might say to a designer or actor, "The script made me think of the *Three Stooges,* only wilder!" or "When I read this, I thought of the paintings of Hieronymus Bosch." Such comparisons express the director's global response to the material without having to commit to a specific production approach.

Should the director say, "I think the set ought to look like a 1950s kitchen," he is not using a metaphor. By going directly to a description of the design, the director doesn't allow for the shared discovery a metaphor can prompt among the other stage artists.

Because a metaphor is suggestive rather than literal, it can be highly imaginative and flavorful, even wacky. The metaphor is a trigger to promote creativity *and* to arrive at a shared attitude toward the playscript.

In the end during the production, the audience may or may not perceive what metaphors the creative team talked about in the early stages of collaboration. If metaphors helped the production be the best it could be in its particular circumstances, they will have done what they are intended to do (see Figure 3.7).

In formulating a production metaphor, examine *at least* the playscript's emotional, visual, and aural aspects. These are qualities that often most fully express the playscript's personality and can lead the director to the formulation of a useful metaphor to communicate her special vision of the play.

The Emotional World

The collective effect of the playscript's given circumstances, its events, and the characters' behavior contribute to the *emotional* world of the play. It includes at least the following four qualities:

- *Value system exhibited by the characters.* What is the moral universe like? Is the world corrupt? Highly moral? Righteous? Morally ambiguous? Religious? Is the world of the play a fair one? Unjust?
- *General mood or feeling.* Is the world of the play a happy one? Depressing? Ordinary? How ordinary? Satiric? How satiric? Warm? Cold? Sympathetic? Is the world highly emotional? Placid? Is the world hot? Dry? Humid?
- *Tempo at which the action unfolds.* Is this a fast-paced, harried world? A leisurely one? Jerky? Rhythmically smooth?
- *Color of this world.* What colors best suit this world? Is the world dull? Bright? Is it a primary-color world? A pastel one? Or, is all color drained from this world?

When these questions are answered, the director will understand much about the playscript's emotional world. Such knowledge can act as a guide to invent an onstage world that will reflect the script's unstated but operative tone, values, speed, and colors.

FIGURE 3.7   From Page to Stage. These photos, inspired by the designer's drawings (Figures 3.5 and 3.6), are from the actual production of *As You Like It*. The concept for this production is listed later in this section. (a) In the climactic wedding ceremony, Shakespeare's character Hymen, who marries the four couples, has become an American Indian Chief seen here invoking the gods on the top platform. (b) Orlando, high in a "tree" with gun drawn, opposes the Duke and his men in the Forest of Arden.

The Visual World

Every playscript has some degree of spectacle, even though the playwright may note that the setting is "nowhere in particular." The *visual* world of a play is always presented on stage in some form, even if the production's setting is limited to black drapes with cubes that represent furniture. When actors moving through space are added to this world, the characters they portray are in a specific place. Identifying and capitalizing on the playscript's physical world is an important step in conceptualizing the production. The world may be a black void, a world selectively realized, or one of much detail; or, it may be highly abstracted and irrational.

Not every playscript, of course, requires the same degree of realistic trappings. Some playwrights create dynamic worlds in which every object must be present; others create worlds in which only selected items are needed. Still others flourish when the world is abstract and nonliteral. Here are some qualities to consider:

- *Atmosphere.* What are the materials of this place? Is the world cold and forbidding and best represented by chrome and steel? Are the textures of this place rough-and-tumble or smooth and slick? Is the fabric of this world voile or sackcloth? Satin or muslin?
- *Abstraction.* Is the physical world of the play literal? How specific are the references? Must a literal copy of the real world be presented on stage? Is this world condensed and abridged? How much detail is required?
- *Focus.* Is the world dreamlike? Hazy? Poetic? How much detail is required to make this place reveal the play's world? Is this a soft, curvy world? Or, a jagged and angular one?

When these issues are addressed, the director will have a basis for developing the look of the stage production. A thorough knowledge of the playscript's physical world fully communicated to the designers will help them create a stage world that reflects the director's vision. It will also help the director make decisions during rehearsals.

The Aural World

The sonic atmosphere of the production can do much to communicate the play. Consider the following:

- *Literalness of the sounds.* How real are the sound effects? Are they called for by the text? Or, will sound effects be interpolated to create a dreamlike surreal world? Is there an aural background that establishes place?
- *Lyricality of the voices.* Should the dialogue sound musical and resonant? Ardent? Flat and harsh?
- *Use of music.* Is music called for? Is it to be interpolated? No matter whether mandated by the author or added by the director, what is its sonority? Jazz? Chamber music by Bach or John Cage? Are certain sections of dialogue underscored? Why?

Decisions regarding the playscript's aural world will establish an artistic consistency for the use of sound during production. This concept is expanded in the following section.

The Concept Statement

Once the director has a grasp of the script's emotional, visual, and aural world, the next step is to translate that knowledge into a metaphorical concept statement.

The *concept statement* is a metaphor. The word *concept* has a number of connotations that will confuse and alienate the beginning director. However, as used here, it means an articulated guiding metaphor that will unite the playscript with the stage production and thus individualize it. The metaphorical concept statement can be the device that communicates to all of the production artists how the director views this script in this production circumstance. It aims to tell the designers and actors what the director's point of view is toward the playscript. The concept statement should embrace the playscript's visual as well as verbal aspects.

Formulating a concept is quite different from coming to grips with a play's meaning. That statement is about the play's inherent content while the concept statement is about expressing what a specific stage production will emphasize. The concept is not extrinsic to the playscript but is inspired by it. Concept is concerned with feeling, mood, atmosphere, sounds, and visual impressions—things that are not easily articulated in a straightforward manner yet can effectively communicate the director's vision and the playwright's text.

The concept statement does not have to be eccentric and startling to be effective and useful to the production team and actors. Although some concepts appear to be weird ("*King Lear* is a man-in-the-moon fairy tale that takes place in the next millennium"), eccentricity is not a requirement for an effective conceptional statement. An effective concept should be:

- *Evocative.* It is not a literal statement about the playscript's core meaning; instead, it should call forth images, feelings, and memories.
- *Provocative.* It should stir the imagination, stimulate the mind, instigate imaginative responses.
- *Illuminating.* It should suggest how the stage production might look and the ways in which the characters will interact with one another.
- *Integrating.* It should make clear how the interpretation of the text, the design, and the personality of the playscript will be communicated.

The director, then, should devise an overriding metaphorical statement to guide the actors and the designers, even if such a statement may seem simplistic. It should communicate the director's interpretation of the playscript's emotional, physical world.

Here are six productions' conceptual metaphors, which may shed light on the phrasing of a concept statement:

- *As You Like It* is Love's mythic fairy tale of the American West.
- *Brighton Beach Memoirs* is a sepia scrapbook of family life.
- *Streamers* is a skeleton of death.
- *Proof* is a fun-house mirror reflection of the mind.
- *The Glass Menagerie* is a look through the cobwebs of time.
- *Baltimore Waltz* is an *Alice Down the Rabbit Hole* adventure.

You may not be familiar with these plays, but the metaphoric nature of the concept statements should be clear without specific knowledge of the playscript.

Experiences

The World of the Play

Using the play you will direct, describe the playwright's emotional, visual, and aural world.

Concept Statement

Devise the concept statement for the first play you will direct. It should reflect metaphorically the play's emotional, visual, and aural world.

▰▰ WHAT THE AUDIENCE HEARS

As a culture, we are bombarded with the visual. Movies and television show us everything. The close shot is at the very heart of film. It is in these shots that actors can act most effectively by silently reacting. We see in their faces joy, heartbreak, jealousy, hate, or fear. Television takes us around the world and brings to our homes the reality of war, natural catastrophe, and human suffering as well as a privileged view of sporting events. If we miss the nuance of a key football play on television because it was shown in a long or medium shot, it is instantly replayed from a close angle in slow motion. Movies and television show us the action of the world.

The theatre can only show us parts of the world, and often the major means of communication is the words the actors speak. Great stage performances have always been characterized by great speaking, by voices that are clear, flexible, strong, and responsive.

Another aspect of what the audience hears goes beyond the playwright's dialogue and how it is spoken; this is the sonic enhancement indicated by the playwright and/or conceived by the director. These nonvocal sounds can suggest the time and place of the action, the emotional tenor of the scene, and the offstage environment, and they can verify the reality (or unreality) of the action. Further, sound can establish geographic location, social and economic circumstances, ethnic heritage, weather conditions, and offstage activity. The sounds of a play need not be limited to the realistic; they can be quite imaginary, fanciful, and/or ethereal.

Orchestrating the aural aspect of a theatrical performance is a major artistic challenge for the director because it is a significant act of interpretation. It goes well beyond the technical mechanics of how sound is rigged and produced.

Sound, whether speech, music, or noise, can be characterized by using the following five terms:

- *Pitch*—how high or low it is on a musical scale
- *Rate*—how slow or fast it progresses
- *Duration*—how long or short it lasts
- *Volume*—how soft or loud it is
- *Timbre*—what the individual quality of it is, independent of pitch and volume

These terms apply to spoken sounds as well as other sonic effects. A sixth term, *articulation,* usually refers to the clarity of spoken sounds.

Vocal Sounds

A production is helped immensely by having a vocally varied cast. The playwright has composed a playscript that is *all words* and most of those words will be spoken during a performance. The script's plot, characters, and meaning will all be communicated primarily by how the words are spoken. Variety and clarity are important. In short, how the playwright's spoken sounds are orchestrated by the director and heard by the audience can greatly enhance (or detract from) the audience's ability to fully experience a theatrical event.

Each actor is unique. Each has an individual sound, a singularity of voice and a distinctive articulation pattern. The director should understand that if the vocal array of the players is distinct and varied, the audience will hear the production with ease and thus better understand it. The audience should be able to tell, for example, which character is speaking by the pitch, rate, timbre, and articulation of an actor's speech. If three actors share many of the same vocal characteristics, an audience will need special visual pointing by the director to discover who is speaking. Selecting a vocally varied cast is an important consideration in the casting process.

For actors to be vocally flexible, they should be able to phrase the playwright's words effectively. The director should realize, then, that they should speak with an open, relaxed mouth free of lip and jaw tension. The actor should be able to articulate clearly, inflect the words and phrases with meaning, manipulate rate and duration, and be flexible in placing and altering emphasis. The pitch should reflect the character, whether he or she is to sound harsh or pleasant. Vocal techniques should, of course, be integrated into the performance and seem to be effortless.

One of the biggest laughs in the great movie musical *Singin' in the Rain* comes when the beautiful silent film star makes her first talkie. She is in a beautiful French period costume, her hair is artfully arranged, and her makeup is perfect. But when she opens her mouth, the words that come out are outrageously nasal and the accent is clearly Brooklynese. Because her physical image is so at odds with her vocal image, the movie audience roared at the discrepancy.

The beginning director must make every effort to ensure that the actor's voice matches the playwright's character. Perhaps an analogy from musical comedy or opera will illustrate a way of judging an actor's pitch. For men, some roles are written for tenors, some for baritones, while others are written for a bass voice. The director may want to consider this when casting. When possible, some players should be in the soprano range, some altos, some baritones, some tenors. If all of the male actors are tenors and all of the females are altos, the audience will have a difficult time distinguishing which female or male character is speaking.

Sound Effects

Many playscripts call for *sound effects*—those mechanical aural enhancements required or suggested by the playwright or devised by the director. Familiar ones include doorbell, telephone, alarm clock, radio, and television. Added to these sounds are the real sound effects the actors make—walking, toasting each other with a drink, scuffling in a fight, pounding a fist on a table for emphasis, the clapping of hands. Sometimes the playwright requires the actors to sing along to the accompaniment of a song played on the radio or a CD. An actor, or group, may even be required to sing without accompaniment.

The sounds of daily life, if effectively and unobtrusively modulated, can greatly enhance the play's sense of reality or its departure from known reality. The director should consider the manipulation of sound effects as another character in the play and "cast" a sound person to assemble and rehearse them with the actors well in advance of final rehearsals. Perhaps the sound person and director can devise other telling aural enhancements, including environmental sounds and music.

Environmental Sounds

Sound can also suggest that the world of the play extends beyond what is seen and heard on stage. Environmental sounds can tell the audience much about where the action is set, the time of year, and the conditions of the world outside the playing area. Consider environmental sounds such as rain, thunder, traffic noises, foghorns, birds singing (or fighting), sirens, locomotive whistles, railroad cars moving on tracks, and crickets. The director can insert these kinds of sounds to underscore the importance of certain moments in the play's action whether or not they are specifically called for by the playwright.

As the houselights dimmed on the Broadway production of Neil Simon's *45 Seconds from Broadway,* which is set in a busy New York coffee shop, the audience quite distinctly heard the sounds of dishes and silverware clanking and clattering along with the general buzz of people talking. These environmental sound effects, which set the mood and atmosphere of the playscript's milieu, are heard again between scenes and before each of the acts.

Music

Music has many uses. It can underscore a desired emotional response within a scene or act. A solo accordion playing *La Vie en Rose* in the background, for instance, may very well conjure the romantic feeling of a street cafe in Paris.

Music (as well as other sounds) can be a framing device used to begin and/or end each act of a play. Music can bridge the gap between a series of episodic scenes. Music can help unite scenes, events, and people, and it can indicate shifts of tone within a scene. Sometimes music is used as underscoring to create an atmosphere while a scene is being played.

Specially selected music can greet the audience as they enter the theater lobby and continue into the auditorium, setting the mood, atmosphere, and era of the production. If the playscript is Neil Simon's *Biloxi Blues* (set during World War II), the music might be pop hits of the 1940s using recordings by the original artists.

In *Vanities,* the action moves from 1961 in the first act to 1965 in the second act to 1975 in the third act. The music played during each intermission of this three-character play can be selected to signify the passage of time required by the author.

Sometimes a composer is hired to write music especially for a production. The director suggests to the composer the style of the music (melodic, dissonant, classical), what the music needs to accomplish, and how long each cue should run. For an outdoor modern-dress production of Shakespeare's *Love's Labor's Lost,* the director requested a jubilant, youthful, and jazzy modern score to underscore the adolescent prankishness of the play.

Imaginative Sounds

Unrealistic sound effects can be employed effectively to underscore or comment on the emotional substance of a scene or a particular moment in a scene. The feelings engendered by these imaginative sounds may be satiric, sad, comic, or tragic. In the final silent moments of a recent Broadway production of Shaw's *Major Barbara,* for instance, the director (Dan Sullivan) used a series of sharp, piercing factory whistles, which accentuated the nonrealistic spurts of industrial steam shooting up from the floor, to warn the audience that perhaps something was not quite right with the arguments proposed by the central male character.

Other sounds used for emotional enhancement need not be this blatant to be effective; they can be used, for example, to subtly reflect the character's interior emotional life. Such sounds might include the insistent (but faint) beating of a human heart, a metal jail door clanging shut, the ring of an old-fashioned manual cash register, or a highly amplified telephone busy signal.

For *As You Like It,* one director had a special score created that included a magical-sounding harp glissando punctuated by tiny bells. It was played when Rosalind and Orlando first laid eyes on each other. This nonrealistic effect told the audience that love was in the air and elicited a laugh of recognition from the audience, thus underscoring the playscript's essential romantic vision of the Forest of Arden.

Sometimes the playwright calls for such imaginative sounds, which can be labeled *expressionistic sounds,* to make audible the character's interior emotional state or distorted perception. Tennessee Williams cites many such sounds in *A Streetcar Named Desire.* The beginning director, however, should not let an aural imagination falter just because specific cues are not mandated by the script. The key to effectively underscoring emotions is to make sure the sounds match the style of the playscript and the production. Aural effects should not, of course, be used in an intrusive, random, and arbitrary manner unless this is the director's intended effect.

Silence and Volume

All sound all of the time is dull whether it be speech, music, or other sound effects. The director should not overlook the importance of silence. Emotional as well as comic moments can be underscored as the characters take a moment to think, understand, or react. The audience may need silence occasionally to take in and process what has just happened on stage. Onstage stillness together with silence is a valuable tool in shaping the dramatic action.

TIP: Locating Music and Sound Effects

Most public libraries now maintain collections of compact discs (CDs). Visit the library to locate appropriate music and sound effects for your directing projects.

Check to see if the music library in your school will lend CDs. At the very least, solicit some suggestions for appropriate music from the librarian by describing the needs of your production.

In addition to silence, the volume of speech, sounds, and music can serve the production by ensuring variety. If the aural presentation is at a constant volume throughout the performance, then the audience almost certainly will be lulled into complacency. The dramatic action, of course, should guide increases and decreases in loudness. As it intensifies, changes in volume help the actors covey their conflicting objectives.

The same guideline should be applied to pitch and rate. Changes in pitch and rate not only add texture to a production but aid the players in expressing the dramatic action.

Sound Designer

The most recent artist to join the theatrical production team is the sound designer. This person is responsible for selecting music and all sound effects, recording them, and integrating them into the production under the director's leadership. The sound person is also responsible for designing and managing the playback system in the theatre, including the effective placement of speakers in the auditorium and on stage. In many organizations, the sound designer is also responsible for amplifying the actors' voices.

The Sound Project

Concentrating only on what is heard in a script can be an important first step in bridging the gap between the intellectual study of a playscript and its life on stage. This experience, The Sound Project, is designed to focus the beginning director's efforts exclusively on the aural world of the production. Using the following steps, the director should concentrate entirely on what the audience hears.

1. Select a very short but complete script from an anthology listed in this book's preface.
2. Cast it with your directing classmates (or others) by trying to match their vocal qualities with those of the characters.

3. Before the first rehearsal, study the playscript so that you have a clear understanding of its architecture, characters, and meaning.
4. Devise sound effects and/or select music that will enhance the script's story.
5. Conduct two or three thirty-minute rehearsals, concentrating on the actors' vocal performance. Consider tempo, interpretation, and other qualities that can be communicated vocally.
6. Perform the script with the actors placed behind your classmates so that the play will be communicated only through sound.
7. When all scripts have been performed, assess the effectiveness of what the class heard during the various productions.

This experience is not aimed at producing a play for radio. It should be treated as a way of isolating one vital aspect of directing that the beginner might overlook. The advantages of this aural adventure are many. Only limited rehearsal is required. Because movement and memorization are not needed, the director's imagination becomes a significant element in the process, and the actors are not unduly burdened by extended rehearsal and performance obligations.

Assessment
To stimulate your imagination as you prepare the reading, and to guide the class's reaction to this first directing project, the following questions may prove useful:

- Do the voices reflect the characters they are playing? Were characterizations fully developed through vocal means? Did the actors sound like the characters?
- Are the voices of the actors varied? Are the male voices all in the same vocal range? The female voices?
- What sounds did the director add to the reading to enhance the text? To what extent were they effective? Why? Why not?
- Did the play seem to end? Or, did it just stop? Was there an appropriate sense of closure?
- Is the speaking rate constant?
- Was the director able to build the sounds of the play, including the vocal performances, to a climax?

Experiences

In preparation for The Sound Project, listen at home to a broadcast or cable television drama such as *The West Wing* or *Oz*. Turn off the picture and just listen to the sounds. Use the preceding checklist to guide your reactions.

Bring a tape of one of the productions of Arthur Miller's *Death of a Salesman* (the version starring Dustin Hoffman is particularly strong) to class. Listen to the last fifteen minutes to hear the climactic scenes and the falling action. Note how the actors use their voices to build tension and then release it.

▓▓ HELPING THE AUDIENCE TO SEE: THE GROUND PLAN

The *ground plan,* a scale drawing of the setting seen from above, is one of the most valuable documents the director uses to plan the visual production. From the ground plan, the director can determine whether the finished set will allow for the effective and varied movement of the actors, meet the special requirements of the playscript, and provide variety in acting areas. An effective ground plan unlocks movement possibilities, making staging easier and smoother no matter what the actor–audience relationship may be.

Because the ground plan is a bird's-eye view of the setting in miniature, it shows on one sheet of paper what is to be placed where. For realistic interiors, as an example, the ground plan reveals where entrances and exits are to be placed, which way doors open, where background scenic units are located, and what furniture will be positioned where.

Ground plans are usually devised in collaboration with the director and the designer. Each should prepare for the partnership by noting the requirements of the playscript (entrances, exits, given circumstances, etc.) and the director's concept and by devising solutions for those requirements. When working together in this way, the director temporarily takes on the mantle of designer while the designer becomes a bit of a director. Both, in different ways, must stage the playscript in their minds by imagining actors moving through the geography of the stage. The designer is primarily imagining the look of the production while the director is seeking ways to express the characters' motivations and needs. When directors work without designers, they must thoughtfully prepare their own ground plans.

Ground plans are drawn to scale, usually a ratio of one-quarter or one-half inch to the foot. Furniture or set pieces (a sofa or refrigerator in an interior setting, an elaborate fountain in an exterior setting) are placed on the ground plan as they will be placed on the stage during the actual production. It is necessary, then, for the director to *read* the ground plan with care and accuracy.

It usually is the beginning director's responsibility to devise an effective ground plan. A study of the playscript's structure will reveal its physical requirements. For instance, directors must decide where and how the climax of the play is to be staged.

TIP: White Models

After considerable discussion with the director, and doing a number of preliminary ground plans, the designer may choose to present a model of the set showing where the furniture, windows, walls, stair units, doors, or other pieces will be placed. This presentation to the director is, in effect, an illustrated ground plan for the production. These models, usually constructed of white cardboard, do not show color or suggest the exact style of the furniture. The director can then focus on the functional aspect of the setting.

TIP: The Size of Things

Granting that furniture may not always be *standard* size due to style and period, do you know how much floor space a standard three-seat sofa will occupy? How much floor space will a standard upholstered chair occupy? A baby grand piano? A dining room chair?

What is a standard height for a coffee table? How high must the seat of a chair (sofa) be to comfortably seat an actor?

There are some dimensions the directors should know to help them read ground plans with ease. A three-seat sofa is approximately 84" long and 30" deep, an upholstered chair about 36" square, an armless dining room chair about 24" square. The seat of a dining room or desk chair is usually 18" high while a dining room table is usually 30" high.

An invaluable tool for a beginning director is a scale template for standard furniture items.

Then they must determine how many other acting areas are needed. Directors must also imagine the architecture of the setting to calculate the most effective places for the characters to enter and to exit.

The placement of furniture can help the director and actors induce movement. For instance, if a telephone conversation is called for, then the telephone might be placed away from the central arrangement of the sofa and chair. When the character, seated on the sofa, decides to make the telephone call, she will have to cross the stage to do it, thereby mandating movement. The ground plan, then, should be arranged to help the director generate and motivate motion.

Why a Ground Plan?

It is at the ground-plan stage of the design process that the director will discover, for example, if the sofa is long enough for the three actors who are required by the playscript to be seated there. Or, if the door is wide enough to allow for the removal of a body on a stretcher by several military policemen.

It is from the ground plan that the director can begin to envision the actors' movements through the set, called *blocking*. Blocking, at least, involves entrances, exits, and crosses. If the ground plan meets the demands of the play, the director will have little trouble devising effective blocking or composing groups of characters that reflect the dramatic action. If the ground plan is faulty and/or does not meet the specific requirements of the play, the director will spend an inordinate amount of time and energy trying to make the actors' blocking effective. If the ground plan is well designed, the play will seem to block itself and the actors will have no trouble improvising their own "footwork."

Changing the setting at the stage of the ground plan is cheaper than doing it later in the design process. Even if there is money to redesign the set, there may not be enough time to make changes to correct problems discovered late in the rehearsal process.

Once the ground plan is determined and approved by the director, the design process can continue to evolve, for the ground plan is far from the finished production design. The ground plan cannot fully reveal mood, atmosphere, color, decor, or line. These production elements can be developed only after the director determines if the production *machine*—that is, the ground plan—can allow the play to function effectively.

Ground-Plan Checklist

The director uses the ground plan to answer key logistical questions about the setting. The overriding question concerns the appropriateness of the setting. This generic question prompts other, more specific questions by which the effectiveness of a prospective ground plan can be evaluated. What follows are descriptions of a ten-point checklist.

Given Circumstances

Does the ground plan reflect the production's sense of time, place, and social class—those given circumstances that are reflected in what the characters say and do? The things on stage and their arrangement must support the characters and their subtext.

Is there enough room for the play's central action to unfold? Can the characters move effectively and easily around and between the furniture pieces? Can the maximum number of characters required to be on stage at one time be accommodated by the ground plan? There are moments, for example, in Neil Simon's *Brighton Beach Memoirs* when ten characters must be seated at one time. It would be foolhardy for a director to approve a ground plan that can accept only eight seated characters.

Balance and Focus

Are the set pieces distributed on the stage so that the audience will know where to look (and where not to look)? A poorly balanced set may force the audience to look outside the frame of the picture, past the outside limits of the set. The audience also

TIP: The Coin Trick

A director wants to be sure that the actors will have enough room to move about and between the furniture and set pieces. An easy way to make this determination is to employ the coin trick when evaluating the ground plan.

An actor occupies just about two feet of space from shoulder to shoulder. To test if the actors can navigate the furniture arrangement with ease, place a coin on the floor plan and move it through the plan. If the scale is one-half inch to the foot, use a quarter. If the scale is one-quarter inch, then use a dime. The dime will represent about two-and-a-half feet in scale while the quarter will be exactly two feet.

Use a coin for each character in a particular moment and move the "character coins" to see what movement patterns can be achieved.

The coin trick can also be used to evaluate scale models.

may tend to physically lean toward the side of the stage that is most heavily weighted (see Figure 3.8).

A well-balanced floor plan allows the director to control blocking nimbly when the production is being staged. The director should be able to read the ground plan to determine if furniture, windows, doorways, stair units, or other set pieces are distributed throughout the acting space, or if they overburden one side of the stage. A nicely balanced floor plan, however, does not necessarily mean that the balance is symmetrical. Good balance requires that the aesthetic weight of the items on stage right be counterbalanced by the ones on stage left.

Adequate Acting Areas

Does the ground plan provide a variety of acting areas to meet the demands of the play? For the purposes of evaluating the effectiveness of a ground plan, an *acting area* is defined here as a place for actors to *sit* (not stand) and play a scene with considerable separation between them, perhaps as much as four or five feet. To meet this requirement, some directors believe that an interior setting for a realistic play should have three major groupings of furniture. This may translate, perhaps, into a sofa and

FIGURE 3.8   Balance. This well-executed white model shows how the stage space will be configured. A savvy director would notice that the setting does not seem well balanced—most of the furniture is on the fireplace side of the stage. Note that because the designer drew the fireplace onto the wall, this element will become more emphatic when a dimensional mantel protrudes from the wall and the fireplace opening is recessed into the wall. The same is true of the window treatment. The other side of the stage, with easel and stool, can only offset the weight of the fireplace side when people stand there. The director and the designer had best modify this arrangement and devise a more balanced sign. Do you see a solution?

chair as the first grouping, a desk and chair as the second, and two chairs with a small table between them as the third. When these three groupings are arranged on stage, the requisite acting areas almost certainly will be available.

If the set is a modern exterior, the same number of acting areas are required. The exterior setting of Wilde's *The Importance of Being Earnest*, for example, might include a tea table, which is required by the dramatic action, with at least two chairs; another table (perhaps circular) with two semicircular seats for a character to write in a diary; another table used by the butler to prepare to serve tea; and a low curving wall that gives other characters a place to sit. During the course of this act, seven characters appear on stage at one time.

In a large-cast play, with perhaps fourteen characters on stage at one time, at least five such sit-down acting areas are needed to provide the requisite variety in playing areas. In a short play with two or three characters, at least three acting areas are needed to provide the director with enough flexibility to stage effectively.

Well-Placed Entrances and Exits

Are the entrances and exits adequate to allow the action to unfold? If the play requires one exterior entrance/exit and three entrances/exits to other interior rooms, are they provided? Do the entrances/exits make architectural sense?

Are the entrances/exits effectively placed for the dramatic action? If entrances are more important to the action than exits, are the entrances in an upstage position so that characters can be seen as they enter? Should the entrance area be elevated to give additional emphasis to the entering characters? Is the entrance area clear? Or, will an important entrance be diminished because the area in front of the entrance is cluttered by furniture?

If exits are more important, are they in a downstage position? This is the best placement to ensure that characters can be seen as they exit. If there is a door, does it open offstage so that the character making the exit will not be diminished as the door is opened on stage?

Accommodating the Play's Climactic Moments

Can the play's major climax be staged effectively in this environment? What does the playwright and/or director require of the physical production for the climax to make its maximum impact? In David Rabe's *Streamers,* for example, there must be enough open floor space for two men to fight and for one to fall to the floor and die. Later two MPs place a stretcher next to the dead body, move it onto the stretcher, lift it, and exit (see Figure 3.9).

If there are not enough acting areas, the director may discover that too many scenes, of necessity, will be played in the same stage area and thus the climactic moments will be diminished because they are being staged in overused areas. If every action unit is acted in the center of the stage, then the climactic action unit, also staged center, will appear no more important than the ones that preceded it. However, if some of the preceding action units are staged to the right and left of centerstage, and the cli-

FIGURE 3.9   Climactic Moments. The ground plan for *Streamers,* seen in this production photo, must accommodate not only the two dead bodies on the floor but the stretcher that the MPs will use to carry them out, one at a time. This moment is the climax of the play and the ground plan must allow for it to be staged without awkwardness.

mactic unit is placed centerstage but quite close to the audience, the climax will gain emphasis.

Can the endings of acts and scenes be staged effectively using this ground plan? The scenes are clearly important in the building of dramatic tension, thus the floor plan must allow them to flourish. (See Figure 3.10.)

Furniture That Can Force Separation
Are there enough furniture or set pieces to keep characters adequately and logically separated during nonclimactic moments? Not every scene in a play is a do-or-die confrontation. Are there enough items of furniture—a sofa, a desk, a table—to make it appear normal that the actors allow the furniture to keep them apart from one another? Can obstacles be bypassed to allow characters to approach one another as their interaction builds dramatic heat? (See Figure 3.11.)

Employing the Full Acting Space
Does the ground plan provide logical reasons for the characters to move to the extreme right and left? That is, through design, the ground plan should make use of the sides of the stage, especially those closest to the audience. Are these areas anchored to the rest of the setting?

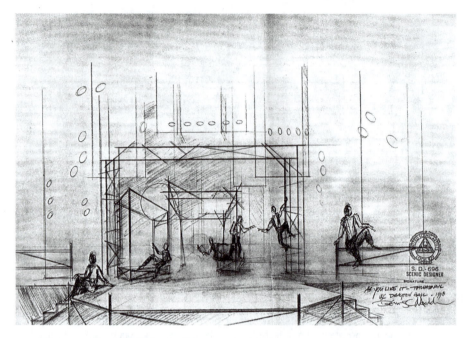

FIGURE 3.10   Sketches Help the Director. In addition to ground plans and white models, designers often provide preliminary sketches of the setting. This sketch for *As You Like It* gives the director information that cannot be revealed by a ground plan. Here the director learns that the railings on either side of the stage are practical and can hold the weight of an actor; it reveals that the structure in the background is also weightbearing; finally, the designer has suggested how the steps leading into the orchestra pit might be used.

Does the ground plan provide logical reasons for the characters to use the areas farthest from the audience? That is, does the plan provide reasons for characters to move through the full depth of the stage?

Using the Stage Floor

Is the plane of the stage floor broken into levels? Should it be? Not every setting requires levels, but levels especially help the director to block plays with larger casts. If an upstage area is sufficiently elevated, for instance, then characters can be staged there without fear of them being covered by downstage actors or furniture. And, of course, levels add variety and interest to the stage picture, while at the same time underscoring the three-dimensional nature of the actor.

Visibility

Clear *sightlines*—the audience's ability to see everything on stage—are important. Can the audience see everything on stage that they need to see? Is something upstage hidden by a downstage set piece? Obstructions are not only physical barriers but

FIGURE 3.11 Separation. The center post of this circular sofa provides the separation that keeps the kiss in this production of *The Importance of Being Earnest* from becoming too intimate.

psychological ones as well. The director should note, too, any audience seating that is far to the right or left. Can the patrons placed there see all of the key action? Or, will the ground plan have to be revised?

Special Requirements

Have the special requirements of the playscript and its production been accounted for in the ground plan? In Ibsen's *Hedda Gabler,* there must be a porcelain heating stove into which Hedda throws an important manuscript that is then burned. This moment is also the end of an act. Is the stove there? Is it positioned so that Hedda can be seen as she burns the manuscript and the act ends?

Testing the Ground Plan

If the questions posed in the previous section have been answered affirmatively, then the director should be confident that the setting will allow for the effective unfolding of the dramatic action. (See Figure 3.12 for example.)

A good way for a director to test the effectiveness of a particular ground plan is to go to a rehearsal space (or the stage itself) and lay out the ground plan using

FIGURE 3.12   Meeting the Test. This white model for the three-character play *The Subject Was Roses* seems to meet every requirement for an effective ground plan. Considering the requirements of the script, the given circumstances are reflected, the entrances and exits are well placed, there are sufficient acting areas in the kitchen area as well as the living room, and there are no visibility problems.

chairs or cubes (and other rehearsal furniture) to indicate the placement of furniture or external set pieces. Chalk a rough outline of the walls to give an approximation of the space.

Once the set is roughly laid out, walk through it, imagining particular moments in the play. If the ground plan seems a bit off, rearrange the space and begin the process over again. Perhaps a desk needs to be moved to the right, or the sofa should be angled a bit more to improve sightlines. This practical (and perhaps private) verification of the effectiveness of the ground plan will save the director from having to make on-the-fly adjustments when the actors are on stage. This same checklist should be applied to the model as it, too, is a map of the stage.

Experiences

Using the Ground-Plan Checklist

Study the ground plan represented in Figure 3.13. It is an interpretation of the one used for Charles Busch's *The Tale of the Allergist's Wife,* a five-character comedy presented recently on Broadway. This New York apartment was placed in a proscenium opening about forty-feet wide.

Using the checklist in this chapter, determine how effective this ground plan appears to be. Why? Since the "specific requirements of the playscript" are not known, ignore that checklist item but apply all others. Discuss the results of

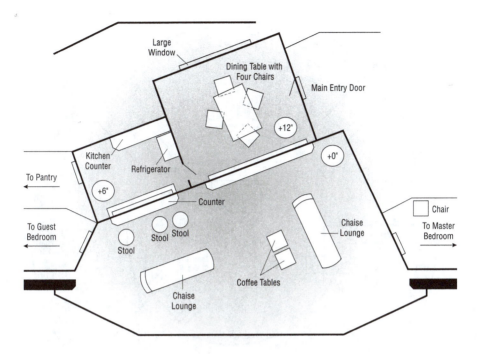

FIGURE 3.13   Ground Plan from *The Tale of the Allergist's Wife*. This ground plan for *The Tale of the Allergist's Wife* is an approximation of the Santo Loquasto one for the Charles Busch comedy, which was produced by The Manhattan Theater Club.

your analysis with your classmates. See also a ground plan and scene from Kaufman and Hart's *You Can't Take It With You* in Figure 3.14.

Making a Ground Plan

Using quarter-inch graph paper, devise a ground plan for *Mae and Her Stories* (see Appendix A).

Measure the playing space you will use to present directing projects and apply those dimensions to the plan. If the acting space is twenty feet wide and fifteen feet deep, draw that box in either half-inch or quarter-inch scale and begin creating a ground plan in the selected scale for *Mae*. When you finish, exchange your completed floor plan with a classmate who has also completed the exercise. Discuss your observations with each other, then share your plan with the class. As a group, discuss the solutions to the *Mae* ground plan.

Again, using graph paper, devise a ground plan in one-half inch scale for the short play you are directing. Then, subject the completed plan to the checklist in this chapter.

(a)

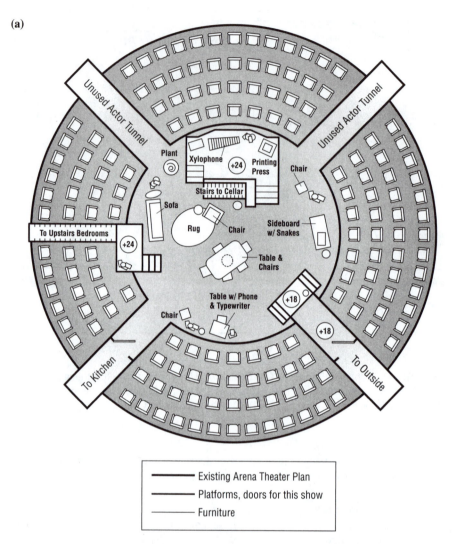

Existing Arena Theater Plan
Platforms, doors for this show
Furniture

FIGURE 3.14   Arena Space. (a) This is a ground plan for the Kaufman and Hart play *You Can't Take It With You.* The designer has invaded the audience space by removing some seats and building over the audience area. Notice how the actor entrance/exit tunnels are used (and closed off). The raised entrance from the outside forces those entering to move to the side to enter the room, and not in a direct line, thus ensuring a circular movement pattern. The placement of the dining table requires actors to move in a circular rather than a diagonal pattern, thus opening them to the audience. The stairway, which goes to the basement under the stage where fireworks are manufactured, further enhances movement. So does the stairway to the bedrooms. The climax of the second act involves eighteen characters who witness the unexpected explosion of fireworks in the basement. (b) The photo from that moment was taken from the twenty-four-inch high platform containing the xylophone. Notice the arrangement of the characters.

(b)

KEY TERMS

With sufficient study of Step Three, you should be able to fully define the following terms:

- Acting area
- Alley space
- Arena space
- Aural world of a script
- Balance
- Blocking
- Concept statement
- Emotional world of a script
- Environmental sounds
- Focus
- Fourth-wall convention
- Ground plan
- Imaginative sounds
- Music
- Presentational production
- Production metaphor
- Prompt book
- Proscenium space
- Representational production

- Separation
- Sound effects
- Thrust space
- Visibility
- Visual world of a script
- Vocal sounds
- White model

▰ WEB CONNECTIONS FOR MORE . . .

These Web sites will help you understand more about conceiving the production. Discover more about the differences between proscenium, thrust, and arena spaces by visiting:

- *www.stratfordfestival.ca* for a look at the theatre spaces that popularized thrust staging in North America; follow especially the links to Festival Stage, Patterson Theatre Stage, and Studio Theatre.
- *www.arenastage.com* will guide you through actor–audience configurations at The Arena Stage in Washington, DC.
- *www.ahmansontheater.com* is a good site to compare the proscenium (Ahmanson Theatre) and thrust (Mark Taper Forum) configurations. Click on Seating Charts for each of these theatres.

STEP

4

Casting: The Ideal and the Real

Casting is always a balancing act between the ideal and the real. The beginning director should know from the outset that there probably is no such thing as ideal casting (especially for directing projects). This is as true in the professional theatre as it will be in the class projects you direct. Although several actors in a cast (whether in a professional, educational, or community theatre) may be ideal for their parts, others surely will be compromises. Even in the plushest of professional situations, actor availability, salary, and billing demands may thwart the best of intentions. What seemed an ideal choice at auditions may turn out to be an idiotic one when rehearsals begin.

Sir Tyrone Guthrie, one of the great directors of the twentieth century, maintained that casting is 80 percent of a play's interpretation. Once the actor is cast, the role is unalterably defined by that actor's personality, physique, decorum, emotional and vocal range, and stage presence. Directors, during rehearsals, can guide the actor to see the character and play it as the director desires, but the actor's basic instrument—himself—is still playing the role. What if that instrument is limited? Cajoling and coaching can accomplish only so much. The director must recruit the best actors possible (see Figure 4.1).

Consider for a moment only the externals of casting. If you believe a character should be somewhat slim with close-cropped black hair with a rich voice but you cast a pudgy blond actor with a nasal twang, then you have redefined the character through casting. The character is now a plump, nasal sounding blond. Certainly there are wigs that can be used, but only in the richest of professional circumstances will a wig appear effective. Although an actor may promise to lose weight, in all likelihood that won't happen. Of course, given a limited rehearsal period, no vocal coach will be able to do much at all to achieve the vocal characterization you envisioned.

▨ OVERVIEW

The director must know what qualities are basic for each role well before the casting session. The character study outlined in Step Two might well be the model for your

FIGURE 4.1 Casting for Look and Sound. The director is responsible for how the actors look and sound. This obligation includes orchestrating the actors' interpretation of the characters they play; devising onstage movement with the actors' help; and leading the actors to create those telling activities that reveal character and plot. The actors in this scene from Lanford Wilson's *Talley's Folly* seem to have captured the personality and action traits of their respective characters.

casting decisions. Identifying the character's action, personality, and functional traits is important preparation for the rigors of casting.

Once you have cast, you have made significant interpretative decisions about the outward appearance of the character as well as the actor's emotional availability to create the character you have envisioned (see Figure 4.2). Casting can also have positive or negative effects on the ease and pleasure of the rehearsal process. The director must be prepared to manage the casting process and be considerate of the actors before, during, and after auditions.

FIGURE 4.2 Character Qualities. The actor playing the central character in Neil Simon's *Biloxi Blues* must have inherent warmth, personal attractiveness, ease, and the ability to project innocence. Judging by this photograph, the actor seems to have brought those qualities to the role, melding his personality with the one Simon wrote.

GOALS

After you have studied Step Four, you should be able to do the following:

- Prepare for casting by summarizing character qualities and traits
- Organize an audition
- Determine the audition process
- Evaluate auditionees
- Understand the audition process from the actor's perspective

■■■ CAST FOR CHARACTER QUALITIES

The director should consider each actor from a number of perspectives. How does she sound? How does he look? What are his emotional capabilities? The director should know the playscript so well that each character can be visualized, as can the ensemble.

Vocal Qualities

You will help an audience understand the action if there is appropriate variety in the actors' pitch, timbre, articulation, and projection.

Draw on the experience gained in The Sound Project exercise in Step Three. Even if you are casting a two-person short play, give consideration to how the actors sound together. This aspect of casting is vitally important whether the play has twenty actors or only six.

Visual Qualities

Consider how the actors' physical qualities match those of the characters in terms of age, demeanor, and height and weight. How do the actors look together? Do they seem to match the characters as revealed in the script's given circumstances?

Emotional Qualities

Sacrifice vocal and visual qualities if you must. But there can be little latitude in casting for emotional availability—the ability of the actor to project the character's internal, emotional life. Here the basic question is, "Can the actor act the part?"

During the casting process, it is imperative, then, that the director discover whether the actor is capable of projecting the essential personality of the character being cast. Is the character's emotional tone light, fluffy? Does the character cry? Scream? Laugh? Can the actor project these qualities? An actor's emotional facility can be difficult to determine at an audition, but the director must explore this issue during casting.

TIP: Casting Notices

To attract the largest number of actors, post notices with all of the information an actor will need to know well in advance of an audition. Include the time, place, date, roles to be cast with a brief description, production dates, and audition procedures. Is the call open? Restricted to a specific group of actors? Are prepared monologues required? Will actors read aloud from the play to be cast?

Notice how these questions are answered in the Disney casting notice for *Aida* and *The Lion King* (see Figure 4.3).

OPEN CASTING CALL

at the Apollo Theatre
for two smash-hit Broadway musicals.

ELTON JOHN & TIM RICE'S

and

Looking for replacements for both Broadway and National Touring companies.

Talented individuals of all experience levels are encouraged to attend!

WHAT WE'RE LOOKING FOR:
- Dynamic pop, rock or gospel singers for various roles including a Nubian princess, Nubian servants, African lions and lionesses and Egyptian warriors. Acting ability a plus.

WHAT TO PREPARE:
- Please bring the sheet music of a song that shows off your voice, preferably a pop, rock or gospel tune that you will sing with piano accompaniment. No musical theatre tunes. Bring a picture and resume if you have one, if not, bring a recent photograph of yourself and a list of any performance experience.

Men and women of all cultural backgrounds are encouraged to attend.

MONDAY, AUGUST 13, 2001
10:00 am – 5:00 pm (sign-in begins at 8:30 am)

at the
APOLLO THEATRE
253 West 125th (between 7th & 8th Avenues)

©Disney

TELL A FRIEND!

FIGURE 4.3   Spreading the Word. This flyer for an open call was widely distributed in New York City. It spells out all of the information an auditionee would need to know to make a good showing. It's clear that the Disney Company is looking for cast replacements, both on Broadway and on the road, for their two hit musicals. After this screening audition, promising singer/actors most likely will be invited to audition again at which time they will read and sing material from *Aida* and/or *The Lion King.* No actor is immediately cast from a "cattle" call.

Source: © Disney Enterprises, Inc.

▆▆ CAST FOR CHARACTER TRAITS

The playwright has given a character specific actions to perform. Can the auditioning actor perform them with credibility? Will there be sacrifices? Can the play survive them?

The author has identified a character's personality either directly in dialogue the character speaks or indirectly in what others say about the character. Can the actor project this personality? Sometimes a character's primary purpose is to contrast in some way with another character. Can the actor provide this functional trait?

▆▆ CAST THE WILLING, COURTEOUS, AND COOPERATIVE

Casting the willing, courteous, and cooperative actor is a blessing to all associated with a production. There is not enough energy or time to cope with uncontrolled tempers, lateness, or other rude behavior during rehearsals. You might consider, rightly so, casting the amiable and good-natured actor over the more competent actor who is a known problem.

Acting teachers can help with casting; they know their students and will want to provide them with broadening experiences. If you are able to describe the nature of the character, they can probably guide you to the appropriate student for further consideration.

Finally, consider casting actors who are at the same level in acting as you are in directing. This situation will provide mutual growth for both actor and director and avoid some potential problems of power.

▆▆ PROCEDURES

Casting procedures vary greatly. Most trained actors have audition monologues prepared and memorized as part of their working tools. Other, less well-trained actors may show up with nothing prepared. The beginning director should be ready for beginning actors by having enough copies of audition scenes available.

Open Call

The open call auditions, often referred to as "cattle calls" by professional actors, are open to all comers regardless of experience or professional union status. Open calls deliver the largest number of auditionees. Usually, the actor is given three or four minutes to deliver a prepared monologue or to read one from the play.

Restricted Call

Some auditions are restricted to a certain group of actors. Some professional theatres invite only Actors' Equity Association members to audition, for example, while others invite only nonunion actors to audition.

College and university theatres often have certain restrictions on who can audition for plays and musicals. Some require that all who audition be students, while others restrict those eligible to audition to department majors.

Whether for professional or educational productions, most often restricted calls also require the actor to deliver a prepared monologue.

Invitation

It is not unusual for actors to be invited to join a production without auditioning. In the professional theatre, important stars are seldom required to audition; they are cast by the producer and become an important consideration in raising money to produce the play.

The beginning director can follow this professional model by deciding to work with friends, inviting them to play a certain part without a formal audition.

Interview

In this instance, the director discusses the part they are being considered for with the actors to discover if they are in agreement on basic interpretation. If there is agreement, the actor is cast. Sometimes the process is a combination of the invitation–interview method, or of an audition–interview.

Callbacks

When many actors turn out for an audition, there is an expectation that the first reading will be a screening audition in which the actors use a prepared monologue. At this stage of the casting process, the director only superficially assesses the actors' qualities. If the director likes what an actor looks and sounds like, that actor is called back for an in-depth audition at which he reads from the playscript. In addition to the reading, the director also may interview the actor.

When calling actors for the second audition, be prepared to devote time to the process. Make sure all actors called back have a chance to read whichever part they wish from the script regardless of whether you are interested in casting them for that particular part. The actors believe you are interested in casting them, and they want to give you their best effort.

Finally, make sure you have a tentative rehearsal schedule for the actors to see, or be sure to have the actors give *conflicts*—times when they are *not* available for rehearsals. It's no use casting student actors who work thirty hours a week, are carrying eighteen credits of coursework, and must go home every weekend, because you won't be able to rehearse with them!

■ ETIQUETTE

When an actor comes to an audition, she has donated time and made an effort to offer the production the best and widest choice of talent available. Actors do this for free!

Their time is valuable, yet they have volunteered to spend a significant portion of it with the director. This situation is especially true in community and educational theatres, as there will be no pay even if the actor is cast. In the professional theatre, the actor may have spent a good bit of money to travel to the audition. All of these circumstances mandate that the director and the production team treat auditionees with respect and courtesy. Here are six guidelines:

- *Preparing.* Explain to the assembled group of actors how the audition will be conducted and what is expected of them—let them know the ground rules. When will decisions be made? Will all actors be called back whether or not they got a part, or will a cast list be posted by a particular date and time?
- *Greeting.* As each actor enters the room to audition, thank him or her again for setting aside the time to audition for the production.
- *Meeting.* Introduce yourself and every member of the production team in the room.
- *Attending.* Make sure every person in the room is focused on the auditionee. Auditors should not be talking, eating, or reading. Courtesy demands that attention be paid to the actor. Answer whatever questions the actors may have.
- *Hearing.* Allow all actors to complete the audition process. If you have asked for two short pieces, then hear them with focused concentration, even if you know after a few seconds that the actor is not right for any part in the production.
- *Thanking.* No matter how well (or how poorly) the audition seemed to go, thank each actor again. Do not give false casting hopes. The director might develop a series of positive but noncommittal comments: "Good job. That went nicely." Or, "I enjoyed your audition piece." Or, "Strong reading. Thank you for taking the time to be with us today."

▰ CASTING CHECKLIST

The director's main responsibility during the audition process is concentration. She must focus totally on each actor as he auditions. Primarily this means listening carefully to determine how sensitive the actor is to the "music" of the play. The director also wants to discover if the actor seems to understand the overarching demands of the role.

Because only the director can know the specific demands of the production, the rehearsal requirements, and the performance circumstances, not every item on the following checklist may be applicable; use the topics that apply.

- *Training.* Have the actors had formal acting classes? Or, are they only experienced?
- *Experience.* Are the actors formally trained *and* experienced?
- *Physical characteristics.* How well does the actor's physique match the part?

- *Vocal characteristics.* Does the actor sound like the character? Will this actor's voice fit in with the other actors?
- *Ability to play a particular part.* Does the audition suggest that the actor will be successful in the part?
- *Personality traits that match those of the character.* Does the actor connect with the part?
- *Understanding of the play.* Does the actor seem to know what the play is about? Is the reading sensitive to the world of the play?
- *Stage presence.* Does this actor "take stage"? Or, does she or he fade? Do you want to watch this actor?
- *Past performances.* Have you seen the actor give effective (and varied) performances?
- *Manner/attitude.* How did the actor behave at the audition? Is this a person who will get along with the company?
- *Directability.* Did the actor assimilate the director's suggestions and incorporate them into the reading? Was he flexible?
- *Likability.* Is this someone the director would like to work with?

Experiences

Casting

As a group, decide the audition date(s) for the directing projects you and your classmates are preparing. Devise and distribute a casting flier, decide on an audition procedure, and hold auditions.

Attend a screening audition at your school or nearby community theatre. Ask the director if you can observe the callbacks. Note the cast posting. Would you have cast the production in this manner? If one or two of your colleagues joined you in this exercise, discuss the outcome of the final casting with them.

Professional Casting

Locate a copy of *Backstage* and bring it to class. Note as a group the varied casting notices for union and nonunion jobs. What casting procedures are employed there? How can you use the models found in *Backstage* to improve your casting notices?

Auditions

A standard audition form (Figure 4.4) can be useful. As a group, decide if this one will serve your needs when auditioning actors for directing projects. What important information has been omitted? What is the benefit of identifying the production's final rehearsals and performance dates?

Audition Information

Name
_____

Mailing Address
_____

Telephone   Email
_____

Hair color   Eye color   Height   Weight

Will you accept any role for which you are cast?   Yes   No

If no, please elaborate on the reverse of this sheet.

Production Information

Technical and final rehearsals for this production will begin on _____ .

You must be free to attend tech and final rehearsals on these days; there is a good bit of flexibility in the actual time of these rehearsals.

The production is scheduled for performance on _____ at _____ a/pm. There is no flexibility in performance date and time.

Audition Notes

FIGURE 4.4 Audition Form. This form asks for basic information that will aid the director in remembering the auditionee, allows the director to consider conflicts, and provides adequate room to make notes during the audition. It should be duplicated front and back for ease in handling.

If you have a resume, please attach it to this form. If not, then please list your theatre experience.

Role	Play	Theatre	Director	Year

Please list your full class schedule and other ongoing commitments by making an X through the general time slots for which you are NOT available for rehearsals. Include your work schedule (if you have one).

Time/Day	Sunday	Monday	Tuesday	Wednesday	Thursday	Friday	Saturday
Noon							
1:00							
2:00							
3:00							
4:00							
5:00							
6:00							
7:00							
8:00							
9:00							
10:00							

FIGURE 4.4   Continued

▬ KEY TERMS

With sufficient study of Step Four, you should be able to fully define the following terms:

- Audition form
- Audition process
- Callbacks
- Casting checklist
- Casting etiquette
- Casting strategy
- Interview call
- Open call
- Restricted call

▬ WEB CONNECTIONS FOR MORE . . .

These Web sites will help you understand more about Casting.

- If you cannot find an actual copy of *Backstage,* look on the Web using this URL: *www.backstage.com.* This well-organized site gives you access to many casting notices that may serve as a model for your audition bulletins.
- To find out more about the union that governs professional actors, go to the Actors' Equity Association site at *www.actorsequity.org.* You might find it interesting to look at the various contracts Actors' Equity has made with various producing units by clicking on Agreements.
- *Variety* is considered the magazine of "show business," with daily and weekly editions that chronicle all facets of the entertainment world. Reviews, Broadway weekly financial reports, and other news can be found in this valuable tabloid. Anyone can join for a free thirty-day trial. Use this URL: *www.variety.com* and go to the "legit" section.

STEP

5 Rehearsing

Staging, Shaping, and Polishing

Once casting is complete and rehearsals begin, the process shifts from the pages of the playscript to the intense, collaborative world of the theatre. When this transformation happens, the director is working indirectly through others to realize an artistic vision. The productive management of collaborators—designers, technicians, and actors—becomes a major responsibility of the director.

An enthusiastic, happy team is productive. The director must use creativity, persuasion, and encouragement to make things happen during rehearsals. So, the director *requests, suggests, urges, questions,* and *advises.* He does not demand, threaten, or force. The dictatorial approach is to be avoided, although some professional and highly paid directors use it with great success.

▓▓ OVERVIEW

The six major sections that follow focus on rehearsals: blocking the actors, inventing business, encouraging the actors to discover telling body language, and ensuring that the resulting movement is pleasing and tells the playwright's story. During the later phase of rehearsals, when the actors have their "words" and blocking, the director must work to shape the production so that it has a varied pace within its established tempo. This is the phase when the director works the most to intensify the action by leading the actors to vivid performances. Finally, the director must polish the production.

In short, Step Five is about what the audience sees and how it perceives time.

▓▓ A PLANNING STRATEGY

The director is the one responsible for devising a production schedule that will give the company enough time to do their respective jobs successfully without feeling rushed and forced to take shortcuts. A good rehearsal schedule gives the actors time to explore their roles and to develop characterizations, but avoids the risk of actors getting stale by overrehearsing.

107

TIP : Rehearsal Strategy

- Begin and end rehearsals at the announced times
- Be ready to rehearse at the announced time by having everything set up, including rehearsal furniture and major props
- Demonstrate to the actors that you are committed to making them look good
- Establish a friendly but disciplined work atmosphere
- Be sure the actors have pencils (not pens) to mark the blocking in their scripts; warn them that it is likely to change as the production is refined
- Begin blocking the production by first establishing entrances and exits for each unit

- Then, roughly block action units in specific places, say a sofa and chair for one unit then a desk area for another unit, and so on
- Visualize clearly how and where the climax will be staged
- After the play is roughly blocked in this manner, return to the units and refine the staging
- Don't expect all preblocking ideas to work; reblocking is to be expected and is almost always necessary
- Keep working on intensifying the action

People respect those who manage time efficiently. The director will earn admiration by being prepared for meetings and rehearsals, starting on time, and ending on time. For the beginner, this task might be daunting but it is manageable. The director should begin planning by using a calendar large enough to accept notations. First, the opening performance date should be marked. Then, the director should work backward so that the last dates noted are devoted to the first step. Be aware that this is a planning calendar, not a rehearsal schedule. The director should not expect to decide what will be rehearsed on each day at this stage; those decisions will be made after casting when actors' conflicts can be accommodated.

Keep the following in mind as you prepare the preliminary planning calendar (see Figure 5.1):

- *Study and conceptualization.* Allow sufficient time to select a playscript and study it. This first phase of planning should include time for whatever research is needed. It is during this period that the director should come to grips with the world of the play and phrase a production concept.
- *Organization.* Another block of time should be reserved for organizing the production, including designing and casting. In professional, community, and educational theatres, this second phase of organization also includes budgeting. Beginning directors usually do not have budgets.
- *A safety net.* All directors would be wise to include a buffer period between casting and rehearsing in case casting requires more time. During this cushion, the specific rehearsal schedule should be made up, working around the conflicts each actor lists at auditions.

Sunday	Monday	Tuesday	Wednesday	Thursday	Friday	Saturday
3 Select Play	**4** Select Play	**5** Select Play	**6** Study, conception, organization	**7** Study, conception, organization	**8** Study, conception, organization	**9** Study, conception, organization
10 Study, conception, organization	**11** Casting	**12** Casting buffer	**13** Rehearsal #1	**14** Rehearsal #2	**15** Rehearsal #3	**16** Rehearsal #4
17 Rehearsal #5	**18** Rehearsal #6	**19** Rehearsal #7	**20** Rehearsal #8	**21** Performance	**22**	**23**

FIGURE 5.1   Planning. This calendar might represent the general planning for a production of an eight-minute playscript with three characters. The great advantage of making a planning calendar at the outset of any directing project is that it will reveal when the director is behind schedule. Laments of "I wish we had three more days of rehearsal but I just couldn't decide on a play in time" can be eliminated. If the play has not been selected by day three (as indicated), the director can see that the project is behind schedule and must work harder (or longer, or both) to catch up. Notice that more days are given over to selecting, planning, and casting than to rehearsals. Such a calendar can be devised for a full-length playscript using this model; instead of dealing with days, planning for a long play involves months.

- *A useful guideline.* As a rule of thumb, allot one hour of rehearsal time for every minute of playing time. If your short play runs about eleven minutes, then schedule about eleven hours of rehearsal. Notice how many hours of rehearsals are allotted to the mainstage productions at your school. Does this general rule hold true?
- *Distribute the rehearsal time.* Spread rehearsals over time. If the production is to be 130 minutes long (not counting intermissions), spread the rehearsals over six weeks. If you are rehearsing a ten-minute play, schedule rehearsals over two weeks. This will give the actors time to assimilate their roles and learn lines.

THE REHEARSAL PROCESS

Rehearsing is primarily about the actors. They are the ones who will communicate the playscript to the audience. The rehearsal schedule must lead them to explore the script and its possibilities, to experiment with character choices, to become confident enough to personalize the characters, and to develop relationships with the other actors/characters. These goals can be accomplished if the director respects the actors and their individual needs.

Scheduling

Generally the rehearsal schedule is divided into thirds. The first third of the rehearsals is devoted to acquainting the actors with the script (and each other) and with the production team. The play is read and discussed. The director explains his approach to the play. Strange words are defined and an acceptable pronunciation is fixed. Unfamiliar references are clarified. This phase is called *table work*—its name is taken from the fact that usually the actors and production team are seated around a table for discussions and readings. Next, the play is staged using rehearsal furniture.

During the second third of rehearsals, the actors learn their lines and blocking. Stagger the times that the actors are to have lines memorized. In a long production, first-act lines might be due on a Monday and second-act lines the following Monday. In a short play, the first half of the lines might be due at one rehearsal and the second half two or three rehearsals later. All through this period, the director should work to intensify the action. It is during the second phase of rehearsals that the actors explore characterizations and relationships. It may be difficult, but the director must give the actors room to experiment.

During the final third of rehearsals, technical aspects are added as the director continues to coach actors. Then it's polishing time. This includes using real properties (including food and drink, if required) and sound. For the final rehearsals, include costumes as well. Try to have at least two rehearsals in the actual performance space; the more rehearsals in the performance space, the better.

Get Help

Directors are helped immensely if they have interested and dedicated assistants. Even for the projects suggested here, the director should gather a production team that can help manage rehearsals, props, and set pieces. At the very least, an assistant will be needed to hold the prompt book and to cue actors when they are working to memo-

---

TIP: Look for the Action

During the early stages of rehearsal, refrain from giving the actor technical directions such as "speak up," "say that faster," or "make that bigger," or "be more intense." This kind of directing is focused on the exterior of the performance and, as such, distracts the actors from concentrating on the interior life of the characters. Technical directions can often lead the actors to give generalized, surface performances.

The director, at beginning rehearsals, should concentrate on helping the actor find the character's dramatic action almost to the exclusion of other staging aspects. If the blocking needs adjustment, phrase the direction in terms of the character's wants and needs.

rize lines; then, the director will be free to watch what the actors are playing. If a class in stage management is being offered, arrangements might be made for those students to help manage the directing projects.

◼ GOALS

When you have studied Step Five, you should be able to do the following:

- Construct a productive rehearsal schedule
- Understand standard stage terminology
- Describe the function of movement in staging a play
- Distinguish between composition and picturization
- Name and understand the elements of focus in blocking
- Identify sources of movement
- Distinguish between symmetrical and asymmetrical balance in a stage composition
- Ground a stage picture using the technique of solidity
- Experiment with inherent strong and weak stage areas
- Manipulate the inherent values in stage positions
- Name some approaches to blocking
- Suggest ways for actors to learn words
- Describe what comprises the shape of a production
- Distinguish between tempo and pace
- Help actors use effective body language
- Lead actors to enliven their performances by exploring choices of playable objectives through side-coaching and other rehearsal techniques
- Identify and remedy indicating
- Polish the action
- Describe some specific rehearsal goals for final run-throughs

◼ STAGE BASICS

A shared understanding of stage terminology will allow the actors and the director to communicate with one another conveniently and accurately. What follows is not an exhaustive examination of stage nomenclature but rather a basic introduction to words and phrases that are used most often.

The Proscenium Stage

In the proscenium actor–audience relationship, directions given to the actor are based on the actors' right or left as they face the audience, not the director's. The area of the stage farthest from the audience is called *upstage,* while the stage area closest to the audience is called *downstage.* The stage floor is divided into nine areas with each area labeled, as shown in Figure 5.2a. Hence the figure in the area marked UR is *upstage right.*

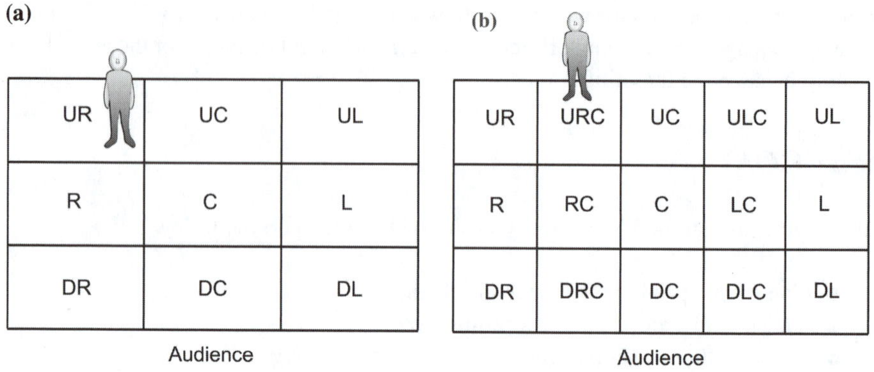

(a)   (b)

UR	UC	UL
R	C	L
DR	DC	DL

Audience

UR	URC	UC	ULC	UL
R	RC	C	LC	L
DR	DRC	DC	DLC	DL

Audience

FIGURE 5.2   Giving Directions. The stage floor can be divided into either nine areas (a) or fifteen (b).

Some directors who like a more detailed breakdown in stage geography divide the stage floor into fifteen areas. In Figure 5.2b, the person in the area marked URC is *upstage right of center* while UR indicates the area is even farther to the right of URC.

The Actors

The director and the actor must be aware that spatial relationships convey meaning to the audience. This concept will be expanded later in Step Five. For now it is imperative to realize that an actor's position in relation to other actors, to stage areas, and to the audience signifies meaning and context for the dramatic action.

Six Basic Positions
The basic standing positions an actor assumes on stage can be reduced to six. All relate to the degree of the actor's visibility.

- ■ *Open.* If the actor is facing the audience directly, the position is referred to as *open* (see Figure 5.3).
- ■ *Closed.* If the actor faces upstage, the position is *closed.*
- ■ *Half open.* If the actor is in profile to the audience, the position is called *half open.*
- ■ *Three-quarters open.* If the actor is in a *three-quarters open* position, he also may face slightly right or left (see Figure 5.4).
- ■ *Three-quarters closed.* If the actor is facing slightly upstage toward another actor, the position is called *three-quarters closed.*
- ■ *Shared.* If two actors face each other, they *share* the scene because they are equally visible to the audience. They both may be three-quarters or half open.

The guiding principle is that the audience will focus on those whom it can see best, all other things being equal.

FIGURE 5.3   Full Open Position. If the actor were to turn around and face upstage, he would be in a full closed position. Based on the open and closed positions, when the actor is asked to "open up," the director wants the actor to face the audience a bit more. If the request is to "close yourself," the director wants the actor to turn a bit upstage.

FIGURE 5.4   Three-Quarters Open Position. These actors are each in a three-quarters open position. The female figure is open three-quarters left while the male figure is open three-quarters right.

Taking, Giving, and Sharing Stage

Using the positions just described, the director may ask the actor to *take stage,* meaning to be as open as possible in body position and to *cross* to an upstage position.

If the director tells the actor to *give stage,* the actor should take a more closed body position, perhaps to a three-quarters closed position from one full open, and to cross a bit downstage to face the actor receiving the focus.

If the director tells several actors to *share stage,* the actors should move to a three-quarters open position and perhaps occupy approximately the same plane of the stage (see Figure 5.5).

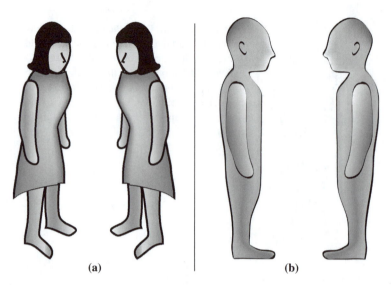

(a)   **(b)**

FIGURE 5.5   Sharing and Confronting. (a) The female actors are sharing a scene because each is in the three-quarters open position facing the other. They occupy approximately the same depth on the stage and are equally open to the audience. (b) The male actors are also sharing a scene but with each in a half open position; this nose-to-nose arrangement is more confrontational than the more casual arrangement in (a). The tension in a scene can be heightened by first having the actors apart from each other, crossing to a three-quarters open position, and then making a final cross to the half open position.

Crossing

Experienced actors who make a cross usually begin and end the cross with the up-stage foot extended. This is a basic technique actors should internalize so that the cross begins and ends in a more open position. Generally speaking, when an actor crosses from one stage area to another, the cross should make a slight upstage arc so that the final position is a bit more open (see Figures 5.6 and 5.7).

    If one actor crosses in front of another, the actor who is being crossed should *counter* the cross by unobtrusively shifting toward the direction of the crossing actor.

Turns

There are at least two kinds of turns on the proscenium stage: a *flat turn* and a *circle turn*. Flat turns are the most common and unobtrusive. If an actor is in a three-quarters right position and must turn and cross left, the actor steps off on the left foot to begin the cross left. From the audience's perspective, the turn appears *flat,* a flat turn is sometimes called an open turn.

    Circle turns are rarer but quite useful because these turns can emphasize a cross. If an actor is in a three-quarters right position and must cross left, the actor begins the

FIGURE 5.6   Taking and Giving Stage. The actor in the downstage position is "giving stage" to the actor on stage left. The stage left actor is open, while the stage right actor is closed.

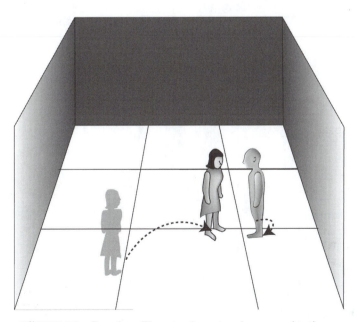

FIGURE 5.7   Crossing. The actor downstage has crossed to the actor stage left by making a slight upstage arc, which allows her to end the cross three-quarters open while the male has closed to a half open position thereby shifting focus to the crossing actor.

cross by continuing to the right, circling upstage, then back to the left. The audience perceives the *circle,* a circle turn is sometimes called a closed turn.

Technique

The techniques discussed here are not do-or-die ultimatums that must be slavishly followed. But, if incorporated into the staging, they will make stage life seem more *natural* because they do not call attention to the way the movement is being carried out. Instead, these techniques suggest an unobtrusive flow of characters through the geography of the setting. If the production calls for awkwardness, then another strategy must be employed.

Prompt Book Shorthand

Armed with the stage terminology presented earlier in this section, along with its shorthand notations, the director is ready to make many efficient blocking notations in the prompt book. "Sheila crosses DLC" means that this character moves down left center. There are, however, additional standard markings the beginner should master in order to note staging ideas speedily and effectively. Study the information shown in Figure 5.8 for a handful of symbols that will make blocking notes easier for actors and director.

X	= cross
@	= at
//	= pause
S	= sofa
C^1	= chair one
C^2	= chair two, etc.
T	= table
W	= window
Ex^1	= exit one
Ex^2	= exit two, etc.
Ent^1	= entrance one
Ent^2	= entrance two, etc.
H	= Character's name, "Henry"
S	= Character's name, "Sheila"
$\overset{\downarrow}{\$}$	= Character sits
$\hat{R}$	= Character rises

FIGURE 5.8   Some Stage Prompt Book Shorthand Symbols.

Now, instead of noting that "Sheila crosses DLC," the director can record: "⑤ x DLC." If blocking requires that Sheila cross to the sofa and sit, the notation should read: "⑤ x to S, ⚷"

The ground plan will indicate where the table, chairs, and entrances/exits are located. If there is more than one chair on the set, then number them (C^1, C^2) to make the notations unambiguous. The same applies to entrances/exits.

As you become adept at using these symbols, you will develop some shorthand notations of your own. Use the symbols found in Figure 5.8 as a start, but don't hesitate to experiment. The goal is to make noting blocking and business quick and easy without writing paragraphs in the margins of the prompt script.

Stages Other Than Proscenium Ones

Although the major aim of this text is to introduce beginning directors to proscenium staging, much of what is applicable to those theatres also applies to other actor–audience relationships. For example, almost all of the terms used for the proscenium stage, and the directions for which they stand, are applicable to thrust spaces.

In all spaces, when there are set pieces or furniture, the directions can be simplified to "cross to the table." In non-proscenium spaces, entrances and exits, usually aisles or entrance/exit tunnels, can be numbered on the ground plan. The director then asks the actor to enter "from four" rather than "upstage right."

Since there is no upstage or downstage (or stage right and left) in arena spaces, the face of a clock is superimposed on the ground plan. Thus an actor is asked to cross to "six o'clock" rather than downstage or upstage. (The director should arbitrarily choose the position of the hours on the clock. The numbers have no significance and are just for easy communication.) Arena movement patterns are most effective when they are circular so that actors' faces can be seen better.

In alley spaces, the stage can be divided into four or six areas, each represented by a letter. Then the actor can be asked to cross to "A." In both alley and arena spaces, actors must not hide from the audience by positioning themselves too close to one another. Of course, an effective ground plan that provides furniture or set pieces to force separation will make the "in your face" position less likely.

Figure 5.9 summarizes some major differences between proscenium and other types of spaces.

Experiences

The Stage

Decide as a group whether you wish to use a nine-area or a fifteen-area stage floor. Then ask one or two classmates to become actors. The remainder of the group should take turns directing the actors to move around and through the grid. When everyone has had a turn, replace the actors with "directors" and allow the actors to direct. The object of this experience is to internalize giving

FIGURE 5.9   Comparison of Stage Spaces. Some inherent differences between the various actor–audience relationships are summarized in this chart.

Theatre Space	Actor–audience relationship	Actor's most emphatic stage position	Actors most open stage position	Most effective movement patterns
Arena *The actor is three-dimensional*	Audience completely surrounds actors like a three-ring circus. No back wall	Center of the acting circle	Very near an entrance/exit aisle facing the playing area	Circular movement
Thrust *The actor is three-dimensional*	Audience wraps around actors on three sides like a Hellenistic Greek theatre. Fourth side is a back wall	Center of the thrust acting area	Close to the back wall, in the center of the stage	Up/down movement, toward and away from the audience
Alley *The actor is three-dimensional*	Audience is on two sides like a tennis court. Two back walls, one at each end of the alley	In the middle of the alley	Very near the end of the alley facing the other end of the stage	Up/down movement from one end of the alley to the other
Proscenium *The actor is flat*	Audience all on one side like a movie house. Three walls to play against and to hide scenic mechanisms	Closest to the audience and facing them	Closest to the audience and facing them	Diagonal and side-to-side movement

movement instructions to actors using the stage areas and directions based on the actors' right and left.

The Actors

Using the stage floor arrangement selected for the previous exercise, have each member of the group direct two actors through the five basic stage positions—taking and giving, crossing, and making flat or circle turns. The object is to allow the director to use stage vocabulary to communicate with the actors and to demonstrate the effectiveness of the precepts identified in this chapter. For example, is the "arcing" cross a demonstrably effective technique for a cross?

Prompt Book Shorthand

Devise a basic ground plan, perhaps for "Waiting"—the play example in Step Two. Plan for a table with two straight-backed chairs, a backstage prop box, and a table to the side of the stage with a CD player on it. Note the blocking you would have Jess and John do in units three and four. Since both characters have names that begin with J, use B for boy and G for girl. Depending on the instructor's plans, either turn the exercise in for a response or take two classmates who will play Jess and John and block them using shorthand notations.

◼ WHAT THE AUDIENCE SEES: COMPOSING THE ACTION

If the movement of actors through the setting, called *blocking,* is uncluttered and the patterns of movement grow out of the dramatic action, then the staging will seem natural, easy, and motivated to the audience. The story of the playscript, its characterizations, the relationships between characters, and the play's conflict will all be embodied in the movement. In short, the blocking devised by the director and actors will help communicate the play to the audience.

Effective staging not only reflects the playscript and the production concept but also uses the full stage. Movement, to be effective, should flow through the entire depth and width of the performance space, perhaps even the *height* of the acting space. This ideal, when achieved, will signify that the characters are at home in the stage space.

The movement of the actors through the setting is intended to express two equally important components that work concurrently: composition and picturization (see the following definitions). If a production is effectively staged, these two elements mesh into an invisible whole called *staging.*

- *Composition* is the technical aspect of blocking that leads the audience to see clearly what the director believes is important. It concerns itself with *clarity*— the pleasing arrangement of characters within the setting that lets the audience know where to look at a given moment. Composition is a still-life painting of the stage at one moment in time (see Figure 5.10).
- *Picturization* is the storytelling aspect of blocking. It concerns itself with revealing character, emotion, and motive through movement, body language, and business. Picturization is revealed using movement that goes from one composition to another.

Using an analogy from motion pictures, composition is a freeze-frame of a chase scene while picturization is the frame-by-frame movement of the chase. By noting the distinctions (and goals) of picturization and composition, the beginning director will have some means to measure the effectiveness of the staging she devises.

Effective staging is influenced by the performance space, the production concept, the size of the audience, and the playscript. The audience's expectation, for example, often will match the performance space; if the finished production is played in a rehearsal room or black box, the promise of elaborate scenic values is reduced and the audience will understand it is to concentrate on the acting and playscript. But if the production is staged in a 900-seat space, perhaps the audience will expect more than rehearsal cubes and street clothing.

FIGURE 5.10   Composition. In this scene from *Look Homeward, Angel,* the director has arranged fourteen actors in the stage right area of this multiple setting. Who is the focal character? Why? What elements of focus are involved? What gives the grouping solidity? You should be able to answer these questions after reading the composition section.

No matter what type of space the production is staged in—proscenium, thrust, arena, or alley—blocking, to be effective, should accomplish the following six goals:

- *Blocking should ensure that the actors are visible and audible.* The movement and placement of the actors must allow them to be easily seen and heard. This does not mean that every actor must be visible at all times; however, the audience should never worry that they'll miss something important. In arena spaces, for example, a character's back will be seen by much of the audience. (Actors can perform with their backs: breathing rates, posture, and muscle tone communicate much about the character's emotional state.) In non-proscenium spaces, blocking must embrace the whole stage, making sure that the actors are visible to all sections of the audience at some time during the performance.
- *Blocking should be pointed.* It must direct the audience's attention to see what the director and designers think is important. Pointing comes from movement, the placement of the characters, the focus of other characters, and open stage position. Review Figure 5.9, which briefly describes some of the basic differences between the various actor–audience configurations.
- *Blocking should be expressive.* It must tell clearly the events of the playscript and reinforce the dramatic action. The movement and arrangement of charac-

ters, in short, must visualize the story. Blocking also must create the proper mood and atmosphere.

- *Blocking should be fluid.* The movement of characters should not call attention to itself. It must appear unified and not arbitrary to the audience. A well-conceived ground plan allows blocking to appear graceful; a haphazard ground plan makes it extremely difficult to move actors fluidly.
- *Blocking should be lively.* It must excite the audience's interest and attention, and blocking must aid the actor in playing an objective.
- *Blocking should be varied.* In addition to supporting all of the other qualities, blocking should be varied in tempo and pace, methods of pointing, use of all stage spaces, and so on to avoid monotony. Varied blocking can also reinforce pointing and expressiveness by introducing new qualities or stage spaces at appropriate moments in the playscript.

The trick is how to achieve the preceding daunting goals. The techniques described in this and the following section will guide the director to devise blocking that will help the actors animate their characters and hold an audience transfixed because the blocking is fluid, visible and audible, pointed, expressive, and lively.

Elements of Composition

Composition enhances the visual appeal of the play by using the techniques of focus, solidity, and balance. Painters, especially those of the eighteenth and nineteenth centuries, were very much concerned with these same concepts. How a specific painter arranges the characters being depicted on a canvas is an expression of the artist's vision. While the painter works in two dimensions, the director works in three dimensions.

Effective composition helps the audience notice what the director thinks is important (see Figure 5.11). If the composition is askew because the arrangement of the

FIGURE 5.11 Elements of Composition. Examine this composition by Tiepolo. Who gets focus? Is the focus only on one figure? How do space, line, area, level, and contrast contribute to focus? Is the balance symmetrical, or is it asymmetrical? Why? Notice how lighting controls focus here.

actors is not pleasing, the audience unknowingly may become slightly disoriented and its perception of the action may be muddled.

With a large-cast production, the arrangement of characters is an important challenge for the director. For example, with fourteen characters present, the director needs to show the audience where to look and what to see. Questions such as the following are important:

- What character (or characters) should the audience focus on? Which characters are less important?
- Are the characters pleasingly arranged in the setting?
- Is symmetrical balance more important to this particular moment? Or is asymmetrical?
- How is the acting area defined? Does the audience know when to return its eyes to the focal character(s)?

The projects the beginning director undertakes will surely employ fewer than fourteen characters. However, the concepts of focus, balance, and solidity are still valuable tools when devising stage movement for only a few actors. The director should develop blocking that supports the dramatic action and is inherently pleasing to watch.

Focus

A stage full of actors, furniture, and stage properties can be visually confusing for an audience to interpret. *Focus* is the compositional technique the director uses to lead the audience to look where the director wants them to look (see Figure 5.12). It is a combination of the following eight elements:

- The body position of an individual character
- The arrangement of several characters into groups
- The space around the central character(s)
- The visual and actual line employed by the characters
- The position on the stage of the characters/groups
- The height of the characters/groups
- The use of contrast
- Variations in stage lighting

Through the use of focus the director can emphasize one character alone, or focus can be divided among two or three characters. Sometimes focus emphasizes a group of characters. Who or what gets focus depends on the director's interpretation of a particular moment of text and how that moment is realized on stage.

Body Positions

Open body positions are more emphatic than half open, three-quarters open, or closed positions. Actors who are facing full front are more likely to receive focus. An audience tends to look at those who show more of their body because they are more visi-

(a)   (b)

FIGURE 5.12   Open and Closed Positions. (a) The character seated on the sofa receives focus because she is the most open character. The character kneeling before her is quite closed. (b) When the kneeling character turns, she suddenly is the dominant character, especially since the seated woman continues to give her focus through visual line by looking at her.

ble. You can illustrate this principle of composition by placing three actors in a triangular arrangement. The actor fully open and facing the audience gets our eye, while the half open actors on either side of the full front actor are less emphatic. If two three-quarters open actors are facing each other (or full front), they will share equal focus if they are in the same relative position on the stage.

In short, the body position of the characters signifies importance and/or dominance to the audience. The audience passes over the characters in the more closed positions and focuses on the character with a more open body position.

Space

Space surrounding an important character in a full stage composition is a basic blocking technique used to give that character focus. Ample room surrounding two characters who are part of a larger composition gives those characters emphasis. The isolation afforded by the space gives the characters focus by making them stand out from the other characters in the composition (see Figure 5.13).

Line

Another very important compositional tool, focus through line, is achieved by having characters in a group look at the person (or persons) who should receive emphasis. This compositional technique is called *visual line*. An audience tends to look at the person(s) everyone else is looking at.

If the group, or only one or two members of the group, also extends an arm and points a finger at the focal figure, the emphasis is underscored. The audience's attention follows the visual line of the pointed arm; this is called *actual line*. Used together, visual and actual line can be potent tools in leading the attention of the audience to where the director wishes it to be.

FIGURE 5.13   Space. Notice how the space surrounding the standing woman in this drawing works to make her the most emphatic figure in the composition. What compositional function does the little boy serve?

Area

In a proscenium actor–audience relationship, the following stage areas seem more emphatic than others:

- Center areas are stronger than right and left areas because they are in the middle of the audience's vision.
- The character closest to the audience is more emphatic than those farther upstage.
- Stage right is usually a more emphatic area than stage left.
- Downstage areas are stronger than upstage areas.

Hence, downstage center seems to be the strongest area of the proscenium stage, thus the most emphatic because it is closer to the audience and is in the center of the audience's vision.

Level

The higher the actor's head, the more focus the actor seems to get, all other things being equal. If there are several actors arranged on levels, the one whose head is highest draws the audience's attention.

Contrast

If one or two characters are in clear contrast to the positions of several other actors, the contrasting actors will receive focus even though their body positions may be fully closed, lower than the other characters, and in a weaker stage area. These contrasting actors are emphatic because they appear different from everyone else on the stage.

Body position, space, line, area, level, and contrast are all composition techniques that are subject to the rules of contrast and variety. If all scenes are played downstage center, no scene gains focus through this technique. If actors always point at the focal actor, then this tool is diminished. If the director always arranges the stage groupings so that the focal character is the highest person on stage, this device loses effectiveness.

The director should vary the techniques of focus so as not to call attention to the mechanical nature of these compositional methods.

Balance

Balance is a tool the director uses to distribute the appearance of physical weight throughout the setting. It includes furniture (and other set pieces), the way in which the acting space is defined, as well as the placement of actors. Balance is achieved when the onstage right weight is balanced with the onstage left weight. A balanced stage composition, one that is pleasing to the eye and thus reassuring to the audience, is achieved through artfully arranging actors on an effective ground plan. Combining furniture pieces (or other scenic elements) together with actors' positions, the director tries to distribute the physical weight of the composition so that what is on one side of the stage is in approximate equilibrium with what is on the other side of the stage (see Figures 5.14 and 5.15 from the play *The Play About the Baby*). If one side seems heavier with actors and/or furniture than the other side, the audience may be disconcerted by the skewed equilibrium.

A director can devise balance that is either symmetrical or asymmetrical, as described next.

Symmetrical Balance

When one side of the stage (from center to left) is mirrored rather exactly by the other side of the stage (from center to right), balance is said to be *symmetrical*. Some plays benefit from a symmetrical balance but most do not. This form of balance, whether in a ground plan or in composition, seems to be used the least by directors and designers

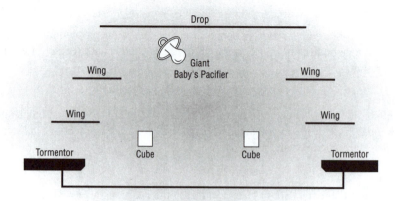

FIGURE 5.14   Balance. This ground plan is based roughly on the New York production of Edward Albee's *The Play About the Baby*. The balance seems symmetrical with wings on stage right that mirror the ones on stage left and two eighteen inch cubes on which actors may sit. The one exception to the formally balanced setting is the giant baby pacifier placed just right of center. The pacifier is practical and during the production an actor perches on it. Does the asymmetrical aspect of the balance introduced by the pacifier make the ground plan more interesting? Why? Why not?

FIGURE 5.15   Body Positions. This moment from Albee's *The Play About the Baby* seems alive and vital because of the interplay of focus, body language, and composition. The woman seated on the cube receives visual focus from the two seated actors who also provide stability. The upstage actor, leaning on the giant pacifier, completes the stability and returns focus to the seated woman. Notice the variety of body positions as well as the gestures used.

126

because it is easily "read" by an audience and thus tends to be a dull arrangement even though there may be great variety in composition within the symmetry.

Asymmetrical Balance

This form of physical balance is used quite often by designers and directors because it is inherently more interesting. Physical balance is said to be *asymmetrical* when one side of the stage balances the other side of the stage but is not a mirror image of the other side. Asymmetrical balance is a combination of the ground plan, the weight of the distributed furniture and set pieces, and the actors.

Sometimes the director purposely wants a stage composition to be unsettling, weird, and thus unbalanced, neither symmetrical or asymmetrical. In these instances, the precepts of balance may be violated.

Solidity

Solidity is what ties the composition to the stage. It tells the audience where to stop looking on stage right and left and to return to the central characters. In short, *solidity* is the technique that defines the acting area. Although solidity is mandatory for a full stage composition, it should also be used for groupings that use only one-half or even one-quarter of the stage.

With only one or two characters on stage, solidity is not an important consideration because the audience can easily and quickly take in the scene and know where to look. The more people on stage, the more important the concept of solidity becomes.

Solidity is achieved by placing characters on each side of the main action and having them give visual line to the central characters. Notice how the issue of solidity was solved in Figures 5.16 and 5.17.

Experiences

Prompt Book

Begin to develop the prompt book for the plays you will direct during the course. Using the symbols presented in the Prompt Book Shorthand section, start the blocking process by noting entrances and exits for characters, basic crosses, and other business.

Check Yourself

The photograph seen earlier in Figure 5.10 is marked with the appropriate compositional elements in Figure 5.16. Did you notice all of them when you studied the photograph before?

Using the sketch of an outdoor commedia performance (Figure 5.17), based on a painting by Tiepolo, identify as many compositional elements as you can. Who has focus? Why? Mark the drawing using the photo in Figure 5.16 as a model.

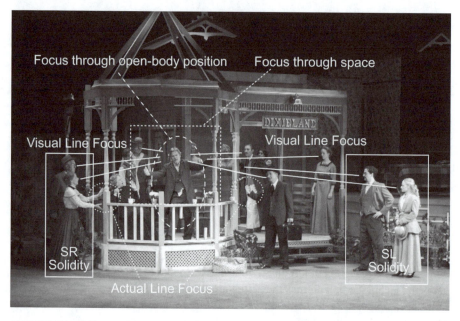

FIGURE 5.16 Composition Made Evident.

FIGURE 5.17 More Composition.

▆▆▆ WHAT THE AUDIENCE SEES: PICTURING THE ACTION

Picturization and composition are the silent aspects of storytelling. Neither is concerned with how the playwright's words are spoken; picturization and composition are concepts devoted to the nonverbal depiction of the dramatic action and its characters.

Picturization and composition together make up the *staging* of a play. While composition is primarily concerned with the attractiveness of the groupings, picturization involves the inherent meaning of how and where the actors move, their positions on the stage, the body language they use, and the business they perform with small props. Picturization is also concerned with the amount, speed, and direction of the movement. Picturization thus gives meaning to a composition that is compelling to watch.

If the director believes an action unit should be titled "A Game of Cat and Mouse," for example, then the director can picturize the element of *stalking* that is inherent in the selected title by the way the actors move, the stage positions they occupy, the gestures they employ, and the things they do with props. For this action unit, the stalking metaphor can be further dramatized by the amount of movement, how fast (or slowly) the actors move, and the direction of the movement.

Stage Areas

Some areas on the proscenium stage are inherently stronger than others, as we have seen earlier. Stage areas also may have intrinsic moods and tonal value associated with them. The beginning director should at least be aware of the relative strength or weakness of an area as well as its associated mood and value when staging.

Strengths

If the scene being staged is one of strong emotional conflict, the director should match that dramatic quality by placing it in an appropriately strong area of the stage. It is not surprising that down center is the strongest area and perhaps should be the area in which a strong conflict scene is staged.

The relative strengths assigned to stage areas have developed in Western theatre because we read from left to right (stage right to stage left); the audience's eye goes first to stage right and moves across the stage to center and then to stage left. A figure in the center of the stage is thus in the middle of the audience's field of vision, so gains maximum strength. Downstage positions are stronger than upstage positions because of the nature of proximity. We tend to give attention to those things that are closest to us.

Mood

Many practicing directors also believe that each of these proscenium areas has an intrinsic mood associated with it. Although this notion has not been subjected to empirical study, the moods said to be associated with specific stage areas have developed over the years through stage practice and historical tradition. Some directors believe, for example, that the up left quadrant seems inherently cold, distant, and remote and is thus an area in which ghost scenes might best be staged. Other directors find mood analysis laughable.

Value

Traditionally, proscenium stage areas are also thought to carry values that affect the audience's response to scenes placed in the respective areas. Matching a scene's overall emotional quality to a stage area's inherent value can heighten the effect of the scene.

Centerstage is said to have strong values; that is, characters occupying those quadrants of the stage are, because of their position, more commanding than those on the right or left quadrants. Centerstage suggests the hale, hardy, robust, earnest, eager, zealous, and energetic.

The stage right areas are said to be warm, suggesting positive values, including friendliness, affection, openness, cordiality, hospitality, and gregariousness. Stage left is often called a cold place fraught with negative connotations. This stage area seems to suggest wintery, callous, aloof, heartless, distant, and unfeeling.

In a recent Broadway production, a modern retelling of the Faust legend, a man sells his soul to a devil-like character in return for instant success. This action unit was followed immediately by an intimate love scene. The director staged the soul-selling scene midstage left. The romantic action unit that followed was staged downstage right. It appears the director assessed the inherent mood and value in each scene and placed them in the appropriate stage positions.

Study Figure 5.18. This chart has reduced the stage into six areas and assumes that it is bare. Do you agree that stage right is inherently warmer than stage left? Why?

Warm Values	Strong Values	Cold Values
UR = 5	**UC = 2**	**UL = 6**
Mood: Scenes that are detached, delicate, gentle, muted, hushed and somewhat detached	Mood: Scenes that are ceremonial, stately, formal, grand, imposing, haughty, violent	Mood: Scenes that are supernatural, scary, suggesting misery, gloom, sorrow
DR = 3	**DC = 1**	**DL = 4**
Mood: Scenes that are affectionate, romantic, sympathetic	Mood: Scenes of direct conflict with strong tension and excitement	Mood: Scenes that are isolated, remote, icy, hostile, detached yet important

Audience

FIGURE 5.18   **A Bare Stage.** This chart shows the traditional mood, value, and respective strength of six basic stage areas. It assumes the stage is bare and unlit. When the stage is set and lit, inherent mood and value may be altered.

Is centerstage the strongest third of the stage? Why? Of course, once the bare stage has been dressed with a set, which may include raised areas, furniture, props, and—most important—lighting, other considerations will significantly influence the meaning of the stage picture.

Lighting in and of itself can focus the audience's attention to the weakest area of the stage and turn it into the strongest one. Up left, for instance, can become a very strong and warm area if it is raised twenty-four inches using platforming with three wide steps leading to it and is also brightly lit with warm colors. Up left becomes even stronger if the rest of the setting is focused toward this area.

Body Language

If the actor's body does not support the dramatic action, then the director has lost one of the most important tools of picturization. Body language is what the actors do with their bodies while still. It is the extension of the body's extremities away from the vertical torso, or it can be a particular body position such as sitting or lying down (see Figure 5.19).

The stage picturization is most telling if the actor's arms, legs, hands, and head all help tell the story. The "talking head" syndrome of the network news anchor must be avoided if a sense of reality is to be achieved. The actor must be encouraged to use body language within the limits of the character and the dramatic action. Motivation, ease, and naturalness are the touchstones of effective body language.

(a)   **(b)**   **(c)**

FIGURE 5.19 Body Language. Notice the body language in these three statues. (a) The archaic Greek statue hardly steps out of its vertical plane. (b) The central discus thrower from the Hellenistic period is alive with motion. (c) The seated male is clearly deep in thought. What story does each of these statues tell?

The visual arts offer a telling example that can help the beginning director understand the importance of gesture. The history of sculpture can be one of tracing the subject's pose from an inert vertical, polelike formal figure to ones swirling with emotion, bodies twisted and arms flailing, and then to more subtle, realistic poses in which the whole body is engaged in telling a story.

Gestures that are mechanical, unmotivated, and only illustrative call attention to themselves and destroy the reality of the moment. If the line is "I called her up," it may be intrusive for the actor to pantomime a telephone by making a fist with the thumb and little finger extended and placing it next to the ear while the other hand punches in the numbers; that is, unless the gesture is intended to be comical.

When Not to Gesture

Beware of random body language that seems only to reflect the actor's nervousness. The director must guard against such gestures whether motivated or not because they steal focus by distracting the audience from the central action.

In addition, secondary characters should not react through broad gesture, thereby claiming the audience's attention, unless the director wants to underscore those reactions. In a shared scene between two characters, in contrast, it is acceptable (and should be encouraged) to have the nonspeaking actor react through body language. This silent communication can, in this instance, help build a sense of reality.

Business

What the actor handles and how it is handled, called *business,* can be a very effective tool to visualize key moments. If a character is washing dishes at a sink, the way the activity is executed lets the audience know what and how the character is feeling. If the activity suddenly stops when a certain line or word is spoken by another character, the audience will understand that something has registered with the suddenly still actor.

The actor and director should collaborate on developing useful business that reveals character and enhances dramatic action. Whatever business is devised, it must never be solely for the sake of keeping the actors occupied with just "doing something." Business should always be viewed as a way to project behavior, situation, relationships, and attitudes. Business that does not make a contribution to the scene should be omitted.

Movement

Blocking may be the most important tool the director uses to signify specific situations, character relationships, conflicts, and story. Movement attracts attention and can be more commanding than speech; an audience watches the moving character as he speaks almost to the exclusion of everything else.

The amount of movement the director employs should be determined by the nature of the playscript. Some scripts seem to demand more movement than others. Important questions, which may help the director analyze a movement strategy, include the following: Is the play one in which the aural elements are most important? Or is the play a knock-about visual romp? Poetic? Or farcical? A *Three Stooges* comedy? Or *Hamlet*?

The director must decide, then, if the playscript to be directed is a *hearing* play or a *seeing* play. If it is a playscript that depends more fully on the audience's ability to hear the dialogue, then movement should be carefully controlled so that the audience can listen more attentively. Excessive, fussy movement can be the undoing of a hearing play.

If the playscript relies more on what the audience sees, then the visual elements, including generous amounts of movement, should be emphasized. Inventive business, telling body language, and clever movement are required for such a seeing production (see Figure 5.20).

The director also should be aware that a single playscript may have a mixture of scenes. Some action units may be visual (best served by strong movement) while others are effective only if the staging is quiet and somewhat static. Kaufman and Hart's *You Can't Take It with You* is an excellent example of this duality; while much of the playscript calls for brisk staging, other scenes are best played with minimum movement.

The amount of movement employed signals to the audience where their attention should be focused. Nothing is more defeating to serious poetic drama than extraneous movement, nor is a farce best served by stasis. The candid shots in Figures 5.21, 5.22, and 5.23, taken during the final dress rehearsal of David Rabe's *Streamers,*

FIGURE 5.20   Body Positions. The body positions illustrated here tell much about the relationship between these two people. Note, too, that the staging places the subservient character in a seated, lower position while the standing character is elevated, and thus clearly in control.

FIGURES 5.21 Focus. The traditional speaker–listener situation puts the listener in the downstage position in order to throw focus to the speaker (a). This arrangement also connotes much about the dramatic action because the upstage actor is a threatening force. Notice the variety of gesture that includes not only arms and hands but body position as well (b).

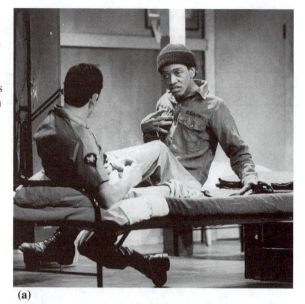

(a)

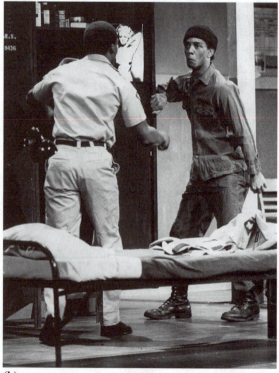

(b)

FIGURE 5.22   Business. Here "Sarge" is engaged in the business of drinking. His body tells us he is not quite sober. Business and body language are powerful, communicative tools.

FIGURE 5.23   Body Positions. The body positions of these two actors picturize the situation clearly. The action unit title might well be "Sarge comforts Richie." The body language each actor discovered tells the story.

vividly illustrate the power of body language, business, and focus. Notice the variety and story-telling that is possible with only two actors.

Although movement animates the play and gives it vitality, it cannot be artificially imposed on the production. Movement must arise organically from the dramatic action (and must be perceived by the audience to do so); it cannot be mechanically applied just for the sake of "variety." Unmotivated movement undermines the reality of a production.

The director, at times, may need to move actors for practical reasons. For instance, if a doorway needs to be cleared for a subsequent entrance, or if an actor must be moved to ensure the focus is clearly on another character, then the director may have to shift the position of several characters to improve composition. At another time an actor needs to move downstage a step or two to be in the light.

These kinds of technical moves, too, must be motivated by the actor and appear to be so to the audience. If the director confides to the actor that the move needs to be made for technical reasons, the savvy actor can invent a plausible movement that appears motivated. If not, the director is obliged to invent a motivation for the actor.

Strong and Weak Movements

Forward movement (an advance) conveys strength; movement upstage (a retreat) signifies weakness. Crosses from upstage right or left to downstage center are inherently strong movements. Movements that take a character back a few steps or from downstage center to upstage left (or right) are weaker movements.

TIP: Discovering Movement

How does the director discover movement? It comes from at least three sources.

The playwright mandates movement in the dialogue. When Brock says to his henchman in Garson Kanin's *Born Yesterday,* "Eddie, fix me a drink?" the blocking is clear. Eddie must go to the liquor table, pour a drink, and take it to Brock. When the bell rings, someone goes to the door to answer it, greets the newcomer, and says, "Please have a seat"—movement is dictated by the playwright.

Movement comes also from dramatic action. Again in *Born Yesterday,* when Billie Dawn turns on Brock and accuses him of deception and cheating (an action unit that could be labeled "The Worm Turns"), she literally chases Brock with charges of fraud as he retreats from those accusations in defeat. This advance/retreat situation is common in drama, and the movement that ensues is embedded in the dramatic action by the author.

Finally, movement can be introduced by the director to enliven a scene. In a long, static scene, perhaps one in which exposition is laid out in a kitchen setting, the director may ask that coffee be served even though this bit of action is not mentioned in the script. Or, movement can be inserted by the director to emphasize telling movements of character and/or plot. The movement introduced by the director must, however, seem to come from the character and the situation.

A careful study of the script will lead the director to unlock the sources of movement.

Strong and *weak movements* carry no preferential connotation. Sometimes an actor is playing "attack" (or "destroy their silly complacency"); in such instances, a strong movement is called for. Later, that same actor might be playing "escape" (or "get away from these unfounded accusations"); in these circumstances, a weak movement is appropriate.

Movement, both strong and weak, is a tool the director uses to visualize the dramatic action. Even if the movement is for a technical reason (to make sure an entrance is clear so that another character can make a clean entry, for example), all movement must be motivated by the actor and appear motivated to the audience.

Specific Uses of Movement

Movement is a powerful tool waiting for the director to make use of it. The acceleration of movement in both speed and duration can help build a scene's intensity to a climax. A bold cross by one actor while others are still can signal a major character's change in objective. A general change in the stage picture, for example, may help punctuate a transition. A flurry of crosses and then sudden stillness brings focus to key dialogue, the character revelation, or an important plotline that follows the stillness.

The three precepts here may facilitate the director's use of movement:

- If the movement (and/or gesture) comes on the spoken line, the movement is somewhat more significant than the line.
- If the movement (and/or gesture) comes before the line, the line is emphasized.
- If the movement (and/or gesture) comes after the line, the movement is emphasized.

When Not to Move

Because the audience finds movement so arresting, there are times when stillness is appropriate. The following are some guidelines:

- Don't have actors crossing while another actor is speaking unless you want to take focus away from the speaking actor.
- Limit a speaking character's movement while speaking because it may distract from the words.
- Important lines may not be clearly understood if the actor says them while moving.
- Don't permit business while another actor is speaking unless you want to direct the audience's attention to the business.

Business and Movement Create Meaning

The Prologue of this book begins with the assertion that everything that happens in the theatre and on stage has meaning for an audience. This is especially true of the manner in which the characters are staged, including the space that separates them (or does not), the kinds of activities they are engaged in, and the nature and direction of stage movements. Staging shapes and reveals character and behavior (see Figure 5.24). The playscript may suggest proximic relationships among the characters, the quality of their movements, and the nature of their business, but it is the director's obligation to reinforce such staging by devising additional staging that supports character behavior and dramatic action.

Spatial Relationships

Proximity carries meaning. If two characters are found to be constantly close to one another, one meaning is generated. If they are characteristically blocked far from one another, then quite a different meaning is communicated to the audience.

Kinds of Movement

The direction of the movement conveys meaning. If one character is habitually making weak movements, then his character is seen to be timid, shy, or unprepossessing by the audience. If, however, a character is often seen making bold and constantly advancing movements, then that character's strength is reinforced.

FIGURE 5.24   Properties Should Reflect Character.   When thoughtfully planned and executed, properties become important indicators of character. From a production of Shaw's *Heartbreak House,* this area is the central character's "home base" in the setting. The nautical items reinforce that he is a retired sea captain. The books and papers reflect that he is an inventor and a kind of philosopher. The space is a bit messy, expressing the character's eccentricity. All of the items uphold the given circumstances and provide opportunities for appropriate business.

Business Activities

Everything that the character does on stage has meaning. The nature and type of business a character engages in can convey and/or enhance inherent character traits. The director needs to be sure that the character's business is appropriate and telling.

The Stamp of the Director

The amount and nature of the movement and business the director stages are important parts of what characterizes the production for an audience. If the play has several characters who are always moving and engaged in one type of business or another, then the audience senses a frenetic and restless quality. If, however, the same few characters are rather static with few crosses and little business, then a formal, perhaps regal, atmosphere is communicated.

If the frenetic staging is appropriate to the nature of the playscript, then the director has matched the play's style. If the playscript is more formal and dignified, then the director who fills each moment with movement has failed (either deliberately or inadvertently) to match the playscript's inherent nature.

Staging and Dramatic Action

Staging, a tool used to express and communicate a director's understanding of the playscript, cannot be separate from the dramatic action. As much as a director wants to build a play to its climax, for example, it does no good to have quickening movement and increased rate and volume in speech unless it is tied to the dramatic action and emotional essence of the characters. The audience will perceive the artificiality of such a technical build and the climax will thus not be heightened.

Variety is important in movement, but it too must reflect the dramatic action and conflict of each moment in the playscript. Variety divorced from meaning will ring false. In a run-through, for example, the director may realize that two scenes in a row are staged with characters in each scene sitting on the sofa; there is, of course, a problem of variety. To solve the problem, the director not only makes the two scenes different in blocking, but he makes the scenes different because of *something* in the playscript and/or production concept.

TIP: Speaker–Listener Situations

When the playscript requires one character to speak at length to another character (or several characters), the effective director will find a way to place the speaker in the upstage position and the listeners in the downstage position. This blocking arrangement gives focus to the speaker.

If the situation then reverses and a listener takes the focus and speaks for a significant amount of time, then the director must find a way to block the new speaker in an upstage position.

This speaker–listener strategy is a basic directing tool.

Business can aid director, actor, and audience to understand the dramatic action, but business, like the other elements of staging, must be integrated into the dramatic action; otherwise, it will be rejected by the audience and seem extraneous.

The dramatic action must propel the director's staging choices; she must perceive the technical needs for staging and merge them with the dramatic action. In rehearsal, for example, a scene may seem flat; the director may choose to insert movement or business to enliven this particular moment. To do so effectively, however, the right motivations must be found in the playscript to support the new staging.

If, during rehearsal, a piece of movement or business seems forced or arbitrary, the director should work with the actors to join the staging to the playscript (and/or concept) or the movement must be changed. In the best productions, the director's contribution is wedded to the overriding concept through this process. The director's hand, in such an instance, becomes invisible. (See Figure 5.25.)

FIGURE 5.25 Working Together. This classic scene from R. B. Sheridan's comedy, *School for Scandal,* requires the cooperation of three actors to execute the business that has become traditional with this production. The taller male character notices that the woman hidden behind the screen has been revealing herself. When the husband of the hiding lady turns in the direction of the screen, his face is moved by the other actor to face front in order to prevent him from discovering his wife in the other's lodgings. This business is repeated several times until, at last, the screen tips forward and all is revealed. Even though the business may seem obvious, it is especially effective with audiences. Sheridan built the scene around it and the actors and director must make sure that the timing is precise.

When we consider the multiple requirements of directing, they may seem unobtainable. Luckily, the rehearsal process, stretched out over a period of time, lets the director look at what is happening on stage first this way, then that way, always working to get the pieces to fit smoothly and expressively.

Preparing the Blocking

A functional, thoughtful ground plan is the surest guarantee that the movement will flow easily, reflect the playscript's given circumstances, and reveal the characters and their motives. The director should imagine movement possibilities for each of the major moments in the playscript to be confident that the arrangement of furniture and/or set pieces will allow those moments to be staged persuasively.

Once the ground plan is set, the director must decide how to prepare the blocking. Should the movement be preblocked—that is, invented solely by the director and noted in the prompt script before the first staging rehearsal? Or should the director turn over the responsibility of blocking to the actors? Blocking strategies form a continuum, with director-centered blocking at one end and actor-centered blocking at the other. The middle ground is a collaboration between the director and the actors.

The Director-Centered Blocking

This method, also called *preblocking,* requires the director to imagine the blocking in private (without the actors present) by going through the playscript and making notes. The blocking is then written in the margin of the script or a prompt book. When staging rehearsals begin, the director conveys the prearranged blocking to the actors. This method is quite efficient. However, because the actors have less personal interest in the movements, they may find it difficult to be fully motivated.

The director can invent the blocking by using the ground plan and some coins of the appropriate size (one for each character) and move them through the ground plan. Or, a model of the set (with furniture in place) can be used with an assortment of characters in scale; the figures are then moved through the space to help the director decide on the appropriate blocking. This information is then transferred to a prompt script to be used as a guide during blocking rehearsals.

A first step in preblocking is to determine the appropriate entrances and exits for each character using the playscript's given circumstances. This strategy will help the director fill in the remainder of the blocking from these givens.

Collaborative Blocking

This approach to blocking is a joint effort between the actors and the director that takes advantage of the "two heads are better than one" axiom. The director decides on the entrance/exit scheme in advance and lets the actors improvise blocking during rehearsals. The success of this method depends on the experience and training of the actors; neophyte actors may not respond well to this freedom.

Armed with the entrance/exit plan, the director also may decide that a particular action unit should be played at the desk while the next unit is to be played in the sofa/chair area. This guidance gives the actors a framework from which to improvise blocking; they know that they have certain parameters in which they have the freedom to follow their characters' instincts.

Actor-Centered Blocking

This blocking model gives the responsibility for staging to the actors. The actors, having discovered and internalized the given circumstances and dramatic action, decide where they should enter and where they should exit. The director gives them freedom to move as they feel the characters' impulse to move. Eventually the actors must "freeze" their blocking, allowing the production to have consistency from one rehearsal to another. After the actors have established a blocking pattern, the director can make certain adjustments for the sake of composition, picturization, and visibility.

This approach is time-consuming because blocking becomes a group process. The actors, however, will feel that they have had a major input into the production and thus may deliver more nuanced performances.

An Effective Way to Block

The most effective way to block is the one that gives the best results for the director. Some directors think easily and quickly during rehearsals and thus do not prepare much blocking in advance; others need to block the scene on paper before rehearsal in order to be responsive to the actors. It is always more efficient for the director to preblock large scenes because this preparation gives the director and the actors a place to begin the staging.

The beginning director, however, is best advised to use a combination of the preblocking and collaborative staging strategies. The director may have preblocked the play, but the actor has been absent from that process. When the actor and the director work together, they may invent a more telling series of moves.

Flexibility is the key. The effective director understands that adjustments and changes in blocking are part of the rehearsal process. Just as actors move through a process in understanding and communicating their characters, the director goes through a process of refining and perfecting blocking.

Staging Checklist

The director needs to determine if the staging is effective, meaningful, and revealing of the production's core values. Staging is silent storytelling; if staging is successful, the audience should be able to figure out much of what is going on without hearing the dialogue.

So, when the production has been tentatively blocked, business devised, telling body language incorporated into the production, and before the actors are told the staging is set, the following evaluative checklist can be used:

- Does the blocking, business, and body language seem motivated?
- Are the actors empowered by their moves and/or activities?

- Are the characters more fully revealed by their movements and business?
- Does the blocking effectively communicate the dramatic action?
- Is the stage interesting to look at?
- Does the blocking sustain the dramatic action?
- Are all areas of the stage used?
- Is there depth in the composition and picturization?

If these questions can be answered affirmatively, then the director knows that the staging is fluid, pointed, expressive, and lively, and knows that the actors can be seen and heard.

Experiences

Movement

As a group, name some hearing plays. What led you to this decision? Do you know some seeing plays? Why did you label them as such? Are there any hearing moments in the looking plays?

Picturization

As a group, stage six key moments in *Mae and Her Stories* (see Appendix B) as "freeze-frames." Present them to the class using your classmates as the characters. Outside of class, preblock the specific still shots to be presented, make notes, and then take a few moments during class to work with the actors. Show the class your work. After each director has presented, discuss each set of still shots using the staging checklist.

Blocking

Study the ground plan shown in Figure 5.26. It is a rough approximation of the set for Neil Simon's *The Dinner Party,* which was presented at The Music Box Theatre on Broadway and designed by John Lee Beatty. The play concerns three

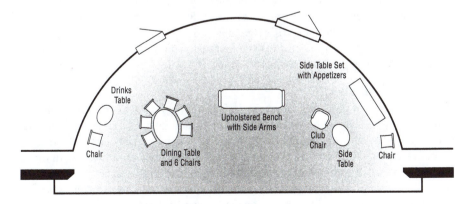

FIGURE 5.26   **Ground Plan for *The Dinner Party* by Neil Simon.**

French couples who are invited by an unseen lawyer to a dinner party in a private dining room of an upscale restaurant in Paris.

The upstage double doors lead to the restaurant foyer and the outside entrance. The stage right door leads to a hallway where restrooms are located; this is also the door that waiters eventually will use to serve the food. No more than six people are on stage at one time.

The Dinner Party moves to its climax as each person, in turn, tells a revealing personal story. Approximate the Broadway ground plan in your classroom. Divide the class into two groups and have each group stage the Confession scene with the actors improvising a story (don't pay much attention to content of the stories). Concentrate on the blocking, business, and gestures. How varied is the staging of each story? Are all stage areas used?

ACTORS LEARN LINES, DIRECTORS SHAPE ACTION

During the later stages of rehearsal, when the production has been staged and lines memorized, the director must give shape to the production. It is only after the actors are confident of their footwork and words that they begin to sense, with the director's help, how one action unit meshes with another and how one scene leads to the next. Shaping the action allows the actors (and the audience) to experience the arc of the production.

Mastering the Words

Learning lines in a timely fashion is important for the actors and the production. Unless they know the playwright's words cold, the actors can only act "What's next?" or say, "Is this the right line?" As a result, the unsure actor is embarrassed and the dramatic action cannot be adequately shaped.

Some actors learn lines easily, while for others mastering the words is a gut-wrenching process. The director should be prepared to answer the question, "What's the best way to learn lines?"; it will surely arise during the rehearsal process, especially from the actors who are petrified that they will not remember. The director, most likely, will be faced with problems with memorization during every production she directs. It is best to be prepared to offer advice.

Protect Concentration

When an actor "goes up" and forgets lines, it is often a matter of concentration. His brain is so overloaded with distractions that he cannot give enough thought to what comes next. The director can help ease this condition by making sure the rehearsal space is clear of extraneous noise and activity. If the set crew is hammering during a rehearsal and an air compressor is pumping, it is no wonder that an actor can become stymied. A peaceful rehearsal space is essential to the actors. Warm-up exercises prior to rehearsal may also help them focus on the here and now.

The director should also consider that while the actor may have been "off-book" when he was being cued by a roommate in the safety of his quiet apartment, at rehearsal he is faced with other actors looking him in the eye, trying to make a connection, or trying something new (perhaps a bit of business). These situations, too, steal concentration and the actor goes up.

Two Strategies to Avoid

Learning lines and cues by rote, in a mechanical way with little regard to thought or meaning, is a strategy best discouraged. Although some actors are able to join the memorized words to the movement and dramatic intent later, one or two players may not be able to accomplish this integration. As a result, the director may be faced with another, far thornier problem: leading the actor to give dramatic life to the words.

Perhaps the worst strategy the director can employ is to call for entire acts (or the whole play) to be memorized at one time by a certain date. This situation can be daunting to the company. Some actors will respond splendidly, others will stumble and become embarrassed, while one or two probably will freeze. Those who freeze may never overcome the blockage.

An Approach

Slow and easy does it best. Integrating the words with the dramatic action/tension helps the actor remember. Rehearsing small chunks of the play, perhaps only two or three action units at a time, helps actors master the words. If the selected units are then repeated with the playscript in hand two or three (or more) times at one rehearsal, the actors are likely to "marry" the words to the movements as well as to the dramatic action inherent in the units.

Perhaps the director can send two or three actors to another room (or to the hall) to work together if they are not needed at that particular moment. These actors should be urged to link the words with the blocking and the dramatic action; the goal of this rehearsal is not to work on rote memorization because the habits learned while "marking" the words will be hard to undo. Instead, the goal is repetition, using the model just suggested.

If actors ask to work alone, then suggest that they memorize in a quiet space while walking the blocking. They should master the first speech, then add the second speech to the first, then do the third with the first two speeches. Encourage them to walk the movement and to play the characters' objectives with the words.

Tempo and Pace

Shape is the result of how the director orchestrates the dramatic action through time. It is the combination of tempo, pace, the volume of speech and other sounds, and movement. When properly integrated and managed, these elements give the production a sense of life grounded in reality.

Tempo is the general speed—how fast or how slow—at which a play unfolds during performance. The variety within the established rate gives the production its pace. (Tempo and pace have other meanings as well, but they are used here with these specific denotations.)

Tempo and pace do not operate in a vacuum. The production's shape also is determined by how loudly/softly the actors speak, how much or how little movement is involved, the intensity of the acting, and how quickly (and invisibly) scene changes are made. The same holds true for lighting changes. The overlapping of scenes or speeches also can make contributions to shape. So can the smooth flow of the production or, by contrast, its sudden lurches and juxtapositions.

Tempo

Tempo is determined by the play's action, the nature of the characters, and the playwright's individuality. It establishes the essential mood and atmosphere of the play. Each production has its own inherent tempo. It is a truism to say that *Hamlet* moves more slowly during performance than does a romping farce such as *Lend Me a Tenor.* What is significant, however, is that not all tragedies move at the same reserved tempo; some have inherently faster tempos than do others. It's just as significant that all comedies do not move at the same heightened tempo. A playwright's script staged by different directors using different concepts can be expected to have different tempos although the words are identical in each production.

Tempo is analogous to a person's basic heart beat—not everyone has the same "normal" one. Generally, a man's heart beats faster than a woman's. However, when a person becomes agitated (from fear, anxiety, etc.), the heart beats faster. Conversely, when a person is asleep, heart rate slows. The same is true of a production; it has a basic innate tempo, but there can be (and must be) variation if its "beat" is to be effectively realized on stage.

Pace

Imagine for a moment a beach scene. You are watching the waves approach the shore. Some waves are strong and forceful, crashing to the shore with ferocious intensity. Others are timid and weak and play themselves out before they make much of an impression. Still others are somewhere in between. But whether intense, normal, or flaccid, the waves keep coming. On a gusty day, the general tempo of the waves is quite agitated and stormy; on a placid day, the waves move at a more subdued tempo. On all of these days, however, the surf has variety within its established tempo. This variety of rates can be said to be the pace of the waves. This analogy applies to play productions as well.

Variety within an established tempo, called *pace,* is necessary to keep an audience involved in the action. If the tempo is constant, boredom sets in. A constantly fast and furious tempo is just as dull as a constantly languorous one. The key is *constant*— a constant anything is boring.

Pace emanates from the director's understanding of each action unit in a play and how one unit works with another. If the director is not clear about each action unit, what it accomplishes, and how it intensifies the dramatic action, then the pace suffers.

Looking at the graphs in Figure 5.27, which show rising and falling action over time, may be helpful in understanding pace. The graphs help visualize the production's pacing, its juxtaposition of various rates of action and dialogue.

Imagine that the director has studied each of the five units of this short play and understands the progression. As the play is rehearsed, the director encourages a rate to emerge for each unit based on the intensity of the rising action. The top graph charts

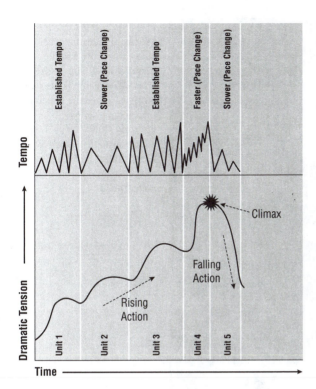

FIGURE 5.27   Tempo and Pace in a Short Play.

the variety in rates that the director has orchestrated with the actors. Some units are played faster than others. Note that Unit 4, the one leading to the climax, is played rather briskly while Unit 5, the denouement, is played comparatively slowly.

The pace, however, must not be arbitrarily, willfully imposed by the director. It must reflect the inherent nature of the playscript. Playwrights build variations into the script; it is part of their craft. It is the director's job, then, to understand these variations and nurture them as the play is being rehearsed. While actors are sensitive to mood, atmosphere, and tempo, they are too close to the action to discern the shape of the entire play. Only the director can orchestrate the tempo and pace of a production. The director is the play's musical conductor.

Flaccid Tempo or Pace
If the pace or tempo seems limp, the director must be a problem solver by examining at least the following four components of the production:

■ *Lines.* It may be that one or more of the actors do not know their lines well enough and are lagging behind the intensity of the moment. Instead of playing the dramatic action, these actors are playing "remember what's next." If only one actor is insecure, the tempo flags. (See Figure 5.28.)

FIGURE 5.28 Knowing the Words. If a leading character, especially Tom in Tennessee Williams's *The Glass Menagerie,* is insecure with lines, then the director's management of pace is in jeopardy. Tom's many direct addresses to the audience will seem aimless and the pace of the entire production will be undermined.

- *Fuzzy action.* Perhaps either the director or the actors are not sure of what is happening in the action unit. The dramatic action is thus fuzzy, vague, and unfocused, and the tempo reflects it. The answer, of course, is to return to the basics to discover what's happening in the dramatic unit.
- *Cues.* A third problem may be that actors are not picking up their cues, so there is an unintentional lag between when one character finishes speaking and another one starts speaking. Perhaps a couple of actors believe they need to process what is being said to them so that they can respond with the proper motivation. The solution is to alert these actors that they must "think" while the other character is speaking. She must recognize the word in the cue-giver's speech that prompts the response and begin thinking (or processing) at that moment; thus, the responding actor is ready to speak on cue.
- *Unawareness.* Another problem may be that the actors are unaware of how slow or how fast they are speaking. They may think they are "moving the production along," but the tempo remains constant; this situation calls for some counseling. A "speed-through" rehearsal may be useful: Ask the actors to see

how fast they can run through the play without eliding movement, gesture, or motivation. This can be an invigorating experience. To use still another analogy, a thoroughbred may not know how fast it can race unless put to the test.

Orchestrating Shape

Tempo and pace must be an organic whole and grow out of the given circumstances and the integrated progression of character and plot. The pacing of a play is the result of the actors being fully engaged in the action. If the director merely says "play this faster" or "slow this down," the actors probably can follow the direction. But, the result may be mechanical, empty, and unanchored to the world of the play.

Toward the middle third of the rehearsal period is a good time to schedule long sections of the playscript so that the actors can begin to experience the flow. If they know who they are and what they're doing, the dynamics of the dramatic action should emerge. The actors will kinesthetically understand when certain urgencies are to propel them forward or when certain disappointments should slow them down.

Volume
Variations in volume also contribute to the production's shape. If the actors are playing their objectives within the dramatic action, the volume tends to increase during climactic moments. In tender, intimate moments, actors reduce volume—but not, of course, below a comfortable level of audibility. Fluctuation in volume also contributes to a sense of reality.

Intensity
Volume and intensity are intertwined. When intensity increases, volume is likely to increase also. Volume is not a substitute for intensity, however. Intensity is found in the character's commitment to the dramatic action. For example, intensity may be fierce but volume subdued; the opposite is also true.

If a compelling shape does not seem forthcoming, consider using some of the rehearsal techniques covered in the next section, Intensifying the Action.

Experiences

Shape
As a group, listen to a recording of Ravel's *Bolero,* a fifteen-minute orchestral piece written in 1928, which has become a staple for orchestras all over the world. The musical theme is repeated eighteen times. It starts quietly with a flute establishing the melody then bassoons join in, and as the theme is repeated, other instruments join. The volume relentlessly increases as it moves to a final crescendo. After the group has heard the recording, discuss how tempo, pace, and shape were managed in *Bolero.* How can these techniques be applied to a stage production?

▆▆▆ INTENSIFYING THE ACTION: THE ACTOR

The director's ceaseless goal during all rehearsals should be to lead the actors to play to the fullest the wants/needs/desires of their characters. This process is called *intensifying the action.* In fact, if the director keeps a clear focus on intensifying the action, the blocking and business will be easier to create because the actor then will use character motivation to independently initiate movement and business.

As the production is being staged, as blocking and business are being rehearsed, the director must multitask. For the rehearsal process to be efficient, beneficial, and interesting to the actors, the director should work toward several goals at every rehearsal. So, while blocking is being devised, the director must focus not only on where the actors are going but also on what the actors are playing when they make movements.

Clearly, during blocking rehearsals, 85 percent of the effort is given over to establishing movement patterns while no more than 15 percent can be allotted to character wants/needs/desires. But later, when there is a run-through of a long scene or act, only 20 percent of the rehearsal should be devoted to blocking problems while the remainder is given over to intensifying the action.

From the actor's standpoint, the rehearsal process should be one of going from the general to the specific. Rehearsals will be detrimental to the actors (and thus the production) if the director is single-minded and believes: "First we read the script. Then we block. Then we develop business. Then we work on lines. Then we work on the acting. Then we do run-throughs. Then we tech. Then we dress. Finally we perform." While these are indeed the tasks that must be mastered, they should not be done in a series. During each of the rehearsal phases, the director, to a lesser or greater extent, must lead the actors to intensify the action (see Figure 5.29).

TIP: Coaching Actors

There's no doubt about it: The success of every stage production is in the hands of the actors. The essence of theatre, no matter what style, is human beings in conflict. Actors must understand the playscript's conflict and must express their characters in action vividly and truthfully.

Directors therefore must be able to work effectively with actors to bring out the best performances. Costumes, lights, sound, and scenery enhance a production, but its heart is the work of actors. Even composition and picturization, which are cleverly worked out by a director, are worthless if the actors do not support that staging and incorporate it into expressive performances.

Thus, a director has two important responsibilities above all others during the rehearsal period:

- To understand the playscript as an expression of the journey of human characters
- To work with the actors to intensify and make more vivid the action of their characters

FIGURE 5.29 Using the Body. The director and the actors must work together to intensify the dramatic action of a scene. In Pearl Cleage's *Blues for an Alabama Sky,* the actor uses his entire body to express the character's unmasked excitement about what is in the envelope he holds out.

The job of intensifying the action is ongoing, ceaseless. At the first reading of the playscript, the director may ask of the actor, "What do you think your character wants in this play?" Later, the question is more specific, "What do you think your character needs in this act?" Still later, "What does your character really desire in this scene?" And finally, "What must the character get this very minute?" The answers to these questions are, of course, called *objectives,* which were introduced earlier. Perhaps the actor will not know the full answers to these and other questions when they are first raised, but by raising them, the director is leading the actor to play specific, actable objectives.

The Actor and Objectives

Objectives are the character's wants and needs stated as active verbs. The director must lead the actor to act on—to play—specific objectives.

The character's main action throughout the playscript is called the *superobjective.* It is the character's overriding motivation. In his notes for *A Streetcar Named Desire,* director Elia Kazan observed that Blanche DuBois's superobjective was to find security. Kazan discovered in his analysis that every moment of Blanche's life in the script was motivated by her need to find a place where she could be safe.

In addition to superobjectives, there are objectives for each unit, for each scene, as well as for each moment in a scene. The actor must always play *something*. The director, then, must lead the actor to find playable objectives that serve the character and the playscript during every rehearsal. At first, this process may appear to be too cerebral. However, if the objectives are clear and actively phrased, the actor can act on them (the actor can "do") in ways that will reveal character, establish relationships, underline conflict, and serve the production.

During rehearsals, the director will discover that many scenes are clearly and effectively acted and that the dramatic action is compelling. The players have instinctively latched on to the conflict, understand the arc of the scene, and are emotionally engaged. If so, praise them for their good work and move on to those moments in which the action is muddled. If the scene is working, there is no need to analyze what the actors are playing. If the scene is not working, the director must lead the actors to find playable objectives.

Playable Objectives

An effective objective has three parts: A want/need, the object of the desire, and the wanted/needed response. The want or need is phrased as a verb, the receiver of the action is named, and the desired response is clear. The "Make Jane marry me" line is clear, simple, and direct. There is a verb (*make*), an object of the action (*Jane*), and the desired response from the receiver (*marry me*).

Not all objectives are equally effective. Sometimes the verb is not compelling enough to energize the moment. The director must be willing to discourage actors from becoming attached to vague goals by asking them "What are you playing here?" when a scene seems dull or general, and then lead them to a more active choice.

If the actor, for example, tells the director that the character's superobjective is "to be loved" or "to be admired," then you will be alerted that this actor is in limbo and perhaps doomed to an ineffective performance. You must realize that the verb is too general, that the object of the verb is not named, and that "love" or "admiration" cannot be meaningfully measured by the character's behavior.

Carefully lead the actor to be more specific. Does the character want "to be loved" by every character in the play? Or does the character want "to be loved" primarily by the heroine? Perhaps the actor suggests, "Make Jane love me"; this objective is still a bit nebulous. Continue working with the actor. If this scenario is

---

TIP: More Verbs to Avoid

In addition to the "to be" verb constructions, there are other verbs to avoid. Some directors are skeptical of the *inform, convince,* and *tell* verbs because they do not seem active enough to furnish the actor with something strong to play.

supportable by the text, the objective becomes, "Make Jane marry me." Perhaps the text supports an even clearer objective: "Make Jane marry me this week."

Sometimes when director and actor discuss objectives, they shorten the process by just stating the action wanted. So "Make Jane marry me this week" might become "Marry me now, Jane!" But the clearer way to state an objective is to use the *verb–object–desired response* construction. This phrasing is unambiguous—it includes the action, who receives the action, and what is wanted.

Actors can't play verbs of "being" because "to be" constructions are not active. Remember that conjugations of the *to be* verb (the verb of *being*) include *am, are,* and *is.* "To be" constructions do not reach out and involve others; they signal that the playable action is directed inward toward the speaker. Thus, "I am sad" as an objective gets the actor nowhere. The "I am sad" statement may be true—the character may indeed be sad, but no action is implied. Action (conflict—the heart of modern drama) demands that a character's motives be directed outwardly to other(s) who oppose that character's specific want or need (see Figure 5.30).

In a scene, if the actor says he is playing "to be charming," the director should lead the actor to see that *charming* is a word the audience uses to describe the behavior exhibited by the character. An actor can't play the audience's desired response. Instead, the director must lead the actor to find the objective (stated as a verb) that will allow him to appear charming to the character receiving the action.

Of course, the scene itself holds the key to a desired action. Perhaps the objective is "compliment Jane," or more specifically, "Praise Jane's sense of humor so that she will like me." Lead the actors to word objectives as imperative verb phrases. Always include the object of the action in the phrase. Thus, "I want to be loved" becomes "Snare Jane!" or "Seduce Jane!"

Lead the actor to translate adjectives, adverbs, and nouns into active verbs. If you ask the actor what she is playing and the response is "I am sad," you might note that "sad" is what the audience concludes from what is happening on stage. "I am unhappy" is not active; it does not send action outward toward others. The receiver of the action is not named, nor is the desired response. Perhaps the more effective action is "Comfort me, Tim, so I'll feel better." Or, "Stay away from me, Jane, because it hurts to be with you now." This might be shortened to "Go away, Jane!"

If the actor reveals that he is playing "sadly," work to replace the adverb with a verb so that the objective is action-oriented and, thus, is specific, clear, and serves the play.

Giving Notes

One of the easiest ways to convey objectives to actors is through specific notes given after the run-through of a scene or act. If the director's notes consistently reiterate to the actor his character's playable objectives, the actor certainly will begin to understand what is needed. The director may say to the actor, "Remember, in this moment you are trying to discover why Mary won't go out with you." If the actor in turn says, "I am playing that," you might respond: "You may be thinking that but I'm not seeing

FIGURE 5.30 Being in the Moment. Intensifying the action includes ensuring that the actor's body language is a significant communicator of dramatic action. In this moment from *Pygmalion,* the housekeeper is intimidating the dustman and the body language of both actors communicates this notion.

it. Maybe you haven't been pushing against her strongly enough to make us aware that you really want to know Mary's reasons for not dating you."

Notes after rehearsals should encourage actors to intensify the action, not tell them what they are doing wrong. "You're not giving me enough here" is a deadend note; the actor may well ask, "More of what?"

Giving notes should clarify objectives and urge the actor to play the selected objective more forcefully or to explore new options. If the director is consistent in her note-giving techniques, the actor will begin the process of making the character more forceful.

TIP: Two Sure-Fire Questions

Remember two verbs—*get* and *make*—and use them to help your actors! When all else fails, the director can combine these verbs into questions that will clarify the action and lead the actors to be specific.

- What are you trying to *get* her to do?
- What are you trying to *make* her do?
- What are you trying to *get* from her?
- What are you trying to *make* him give you?

These questions are not rhetorical. The actor must answer them.

"I am trying to make Jane skip her classes tomorrow," the actor responds. The director asks "Why?" The actor says, "So we can go to the circus."

A playable objective has emerged: "Lure Jane to skip classes so that we can go to the circus together."

Notes also can be given to correct problems such as sightlines or the specific use of an important prop. But the director should be aware that, from the actor's standpoint, these are technical notes. The actor wants acting notes! So, if possible give acting notes first and then the actor's technical notes. Give notes to the designers and technicians first (or last) and then concentrate on the actors. Perhaps the technician's notes can be given while the actors are refreshing themselves.

Making Choices

The beginning director must realize that rehearsals are a process that allows the director and actors to make discoveries, to explore the playwright's action, or to strengthen conflict. Knowing that there are many suitable objectives that an actor can investigate frees the actor (and the director) from the pressure of having to get it right the first time. Making choices is at the heart of intensifying action.

There is no inherently "right" or "wrong" objective, only a poorly phrased or unclear objective that leads the actor astray, or objectives that are not being played strongly and clearly enough by the actor. If an objective is playable and conforms with the given circumstances of the text, then it is worth exploring during rehearsal. It is this exploration that allows the actors and the director to discover the most revealing and effective objectives and, thus, to arrive at a compelling interpretation of the play.

If one choice isn't energizing a moment, then reexamine the choice and make it more compelling, or, select another objective. Remember that the goal is to intensify the action by selecting and playing "dangerous" choices—ones that are exciting and supported by the text.

Intensifying the action though rehearsals is an ongoing process. Sometimes during one rehearsal improvements are made quickly and progress is astonishing, but sometimes progress is slow or nonexistent. If you and your actors are together exploring new choices, or if the actor wants "to try something new," the rehearsal may seem to go nowhere. Or worse, it may seem that the company has regressed. Progress is not always linear from rehearsal to rehearsal.

Indicating

The director must lead actors away from *demonstrating* what their characters want or need. Actors must not telegraph how they feel, who they are, or what they want to the audience in the shorthand of facial expressions, gestures, exaggerated emotions, or physical posturing. Such shorthand demonstrations are called *indicating*. Indicating is not an appropriate way to intensify the action.

When the director spots indicated moments during rehearsals, they are a blatant sign that the actors are at a loss. The actors don't know what to "do" so they "show." The director must lead the actors back to the basics by asking questions such as the following:

- What is happening in the scene?
- What are the characters playing?
- What are their objectives?
- What strategy does the character employ to achieve the objective?
- What are the obstacles (the conflicts) that keep the character from achieving the objective?

The director must reassure the actors that if they fully commit to the action (if they *do*), they will not have to indicate (*show*) what is happening in the scene. The actors, in turn, will discover that they are gesturing less often, that facial mugging is diminished, and that they engage in fewer vocal tricks. In short, the actors will realize that they are giving to their characters the responsibility for communicating the essence of the scene. The actors then will gain confidence in the characters and discover the adage that "less is more."

If the discussion of given circumstances or the show/do talk is not productive, then there are two techniques for dealing with indicating that the director can consider using. The first is to alert the actors that at the next rehearsal they will not be allowed to use their arms and/or hands to gesture. Ask the actors to think about the consequences of this restriction and to come prepared to deal with it.

The second technique involves the use of a mask. Again, alert the actors that at the next rehearsal you will ask that they wear a neutral mask to prevent them from communicating with facial gestures. Ask them to think about the consequences of this restriction. You may or may not choose to follow up on this drastic procedure, but certainly it will alert the actors that they are seriously indicating.

Side-Coaching

During an early run-through of the entire play or even an act, the director may sense that while the production is in good shape generally, some parts are dull. This symptom reveals, perhaps, that the choices of objectives are flabby, or, that the actors are not acting the playable objectives they have chosen with full force. In either case, a reexamination of objectives is indicated.

An important technique that the director can use to intensify the action is *side-coaching*. This strategy is best employed midway during the rehearsal process when the actors have memorized their lines. The director prepares the actors for this exercise by explaining that during the side-coaching rehearsal she will give them objectives to experiment with. The actors are not to break character and are not to discuss the side-coaching, but are to improvise on the director's comments by incorporating them into the scene as best they can.

Once the scene has begun, the director enthusiastically offers comments to the actors in the form of objectives and urges them to act on them. Some typical interjections to use include the following:

- Hit Tom with the news!
- Make Tom speechless!
- Blast Tom with the facts!
- Stun Tom!

To another actor, the director can urge:

- Escape Jane!
- Ignore Jane's lies!
- Get out of the room!

This coaching technique is often used when the director decides the actors are too passive, too laid back, too introspective. It is a way to "up the ante" and make a scene more dynamic.

Experiences

Objectives and Side-Coaching

Invite two actors to class who have already presented a scene in an acting course. They must be secure in memorization. Select one or two members of the group to work with the actors on intensifying the action by clarifying objectives, giving more active objectives, and using side-coaching. How do the actor's respond? Has the scene intensified? Why? Why not?

▉▉ POLISHING

The final stage in the rehearsal process is polishing the production. This phase happens only after the actors know lines, there have been many "working" rehearsals at which the primary goal has been to intensify the action, and acts have been run.

Then, there comes a time when the director realizes that the actors are ready for a new challenge and that further microrehearsing will not inspire them but, instead, bore them. It is time, in short, to take a macroview of the production by scheduling full, uninterrupted run-throughs. The attention of the company should be focused on the whole picture. It is at this rehearsal stage that the director discovers what the production will look like and sound like through time. The actors too will make breakthroughs.

The Actors' Discovery

Each of the several run-throughs should have a specific goal for the actors as well as the crew. The director should share the rehearsal intent with the company so that all can focus on the same outcome. Some important run-through goals include the following five:

■ *Continuity.* This particular run, usually the first in a series of full runs, is devoted to letting the actors experience the wholeness of what comes next. A playscript can be analyzed as a series of parts—beats, action units, scenes, and acts—but during performance it must be one whole thing, bigger than just its parts. Understanding its continuity is important for everyone connected with the production.

■ *Connections.* The actors are asked in this run to work diligently on making connections with the other characters to enrich the texture of the production. They should look directly at the other characters, listen carefully to what they have to say, and react appropriately and freshly to the circumstances (see Figure 5.31). If this behavior is not appropriate for a character, then the actor must concentrate on ignoring and not hearing.

■ *Clarity.* Here the actors are urged to be precise, to explore their timing and phrasing. They are to focus especially on the dramatic action that leads to curtain lines and to play these moments with clarity and boldness.

■ *Entrances/exits.* This run is to focus on having the actors concentrate on where they came from before entering and why they entered. Conversely, when exiting they are to play boldly their reason for exiting and to concentrate on where they are going.

■ *Confidence.* Dedicate this run-through to using as many of the real props as possible to ensure that the actors are familiar and confident with them. This run will give the company the assurance to face the distractions of stop-and-go technical rehearsals that will follow. If the actors gain authority, they will be free to explore the playscript's subtlety and intricacy.

When rehearsals are devoted to uninterrupted run-throughs of the entire production, the director may find that the actors are energized by new discoveries. They can begin to internalize the continuity and make more meaningful connections with other characters. The actors make clearer entrances/exits and are more effective in playing their actions. In short, they will give bolder, more assured performances. "No

FIGURE 5.31   Listening. The actor's face can communicate worlds of information if she is focused on the moment, listens, and concentrates on the dramatic action. These women are discovering that Medea plans to kill her children.

stops for any reason" must be the mandate, however. These full runs are for the actors. Run-throughs can and often do instill confidence.

The Director's Discovery

It is during this polishing phase of rehearsals, before technical rehearsals begin, that the director discovers what he has (or has not) been best at directing. There is nothing like seeing the actors play the full playscript to give the director a sense of the whole and what may still need improvement (see Figure 5.32).

As the actors are accomplishing the specific run-through goals, the director also must use these rehearsals to see the production anew. While the director is always a surrogate for the audience, this role is especially important during full runs of the production.

During run-throughs, the director checks for the clarity of the storytelling, the effectiveness of the climax(es), the production's shape, the transitions between scenes or major entrances and exits, and the quality of the business. The following checklist can be used to assess the production:

- *Storytelling.* Is the story clear? Are all elements of the plot being projected? Is the arc of the storytelling compelling? If not, why? Is the story being communicated with emotional force? Or, is it being told with rhetoric?

FIGURE 5.32   Polishing. During final run-throughs, the director can determine whether everything has come together. In this picture, taken during the second dress rehearsal of *The Robber Bridegroom,* the director checks to see that ground plan, business, body language, composition, and picturization all merge to clearly tell the dramatic action.

- *Characters and relationships.* Are the characterizations clear? Are the emotional interactions between actors true? Are the characters actively engaged with one another?
- *Climaxes.* Are the key moments in the production effective? Are they grounded in truth? Or, are some overacted? Do they accomplish what is intended? If not, why?
- *Shape.* Is the tempo appropriate? Is there variation within that rate? Is the production monotonous because it is too evenly played? If so, the director should look to intensify the tempo.
- *Transitions.* Do the transitions happen effortlessly? If they are awkward, why?
- *Business.* Is the business appropriate? Does the business illuminate character or dramatic action? If not, perhaps it should be cut. Does a new bit of business need to be added?

Perhaps the director can invite a mentor or colleague who has not attended rehearsals before to view a run-through. Later, and privately, the director can ask specific questions about characterizations, shape, and dramatic action. The six areas just listed are places to start the discussion. This impartial sounding board may reconfirm what the director believes of the production. Or, it may alert the director to other concerns. In any case, the observer is not to give responses to the actors, but only to the director.

At one late run-through of a full-length production scheduled to open in six days, a director asked a confidante if she understood an important staging convention employed during the production. She admitted she was puzzled. The director thought about this response overnight and in ten minutes of rehearsal the next day, restaged the production's opening moment to give emphasis to the significant convention. The actors were secure with their roles and with the playscript then and absorbed the change with little difficulty. After the restaging, the run-through proceeded without interruption.

Giving Notes

At this point in the rehearsal process, notes should be written. This procedure will limit the director to conciseness and clarity about what is wanted. The time for extended meaningful discussions is over; the actors need specifics.

Curtain Calls

The last memory the audience has of a production is the curtain call. It should be as well rehearsed as the rest of the production.

Why a curtain call? The answer is tied to theatre etiquette and tradition. If the audience applauds the production, and they will, it is only polite that the actors acknowledge this by saying, "Thank you for your applause" in the tradition of the "company bow."

The director is therefore obligated to acknowledge the audience's response by having the actors take a well-rehearsed bow. It doesn't have to be elaborate, and perhaps it shouldn't be, but it does have to be designed. It's unfair to the actors to ask them to "wing" the call by sheepishly stepping forward in an uncoordinated effort. Rehearsing a curtain call takes only a few moments of rehearsal time. The call is usually added during the final run-throughs before the first technical rehearsals.

There must be a clear break between the end of the play and the curtain call. This effect can be accomplished in any number of ways, even for a bare-bones directing project. For example, the lights can be doused, music can build to a climax, the actors can freeze, or all three techniques might be employed. For the curtain call to be effective and the audience fulfilled, the director must shape the final moments of the production, the falling action, so that the production ends and does not just stop.

Deficiencies

When the production goes into full run-throughs, the director still may not be satisfied with every actor's performance. He somehow senses, however, that he will have to accept what is there and make the production seem as accomplished as possible using what the actors are giving.

Without alerting (and thus demoralizing) the actors, the director goes about adjusting the production by integrating incomplete or wrong-headed actor choices into the fabric of the production. The director, then, tries to mask the production's defects—and there isn't a production that doesn't have one or two.

These shortcomings may include one or two ineffective performances or even a basic miscalculation in casting. Perhaps the director has not been able to lead an actor to make the most effective choices at particular moments. In each of these instances, the director must make what is on stage seem competent and exciting.

British director Margaret Webster was staging an uncut production of *Hamlet*. During previews, she discovered that the "something's rotten in the state of Denmark" line triggered the audience to laugh. She couldn't delete the line and still be true to the "uncut" concept, so she covered it with a fanfare of trumpets. The audience did not hear the line but it was spoken; she had killed the unwanted laugh.

Sometimes it's necessary for the good of the production to obscure an ineffective moment or actor. This skill, too, is part of the director's craft. Perhaps the most obvious solution is to reduce the length of the ineffective actor's part by judicious cutting. The actor is told, of course, that the cuts are for the sake of time so as not to dishearten the ineffective actor. Directors can come up with other tactics to diffuse an unpersuasive performance that are specific to a particular production.

If a scene that is important to the dramatic action is less than effective, that scene must be reconsidered by the director. Perhaps it is staging; if so, restaging is in order. Maybe an insecure actor will be more effective with less movement so that she can concentrate on her lines. Could she be seated and have the other actors move about her? Whatever the cause, the director has one or two more rehearsals to repair the ineffectiveness.

To make changes and still preserve the integrity of the uninterrupted run, the director must rehearse whatever changes are to be made before the run-through begins. If this strategy is followed, the actors get the needed run and the director gets to make necessary changes.

One caveat: The director must not make any changes for the final two run-throughs; the actors deserve the reassurance of uninterrupted rehearsals before the technical and dress rehearsals.

Technical and Dress Rehearsals

Just before the first performance of a production, the final rehearsals are given over to coordinating the acting with the sets, properties, lighting, and sound, called *technical* rehearsals (see Figure 5.33). When the technical aspects are in working order, then costumes and makeup are added to the production, called *dress* rehearsals.

For directing projects, this is a simple procedure since lighting, most probably, will be general illumination in which the lights are turned on to start the project and then turned off at its conclusion. Set and props will be minimal too, but the director must consider them so that the actors are familiar with the chairs they will sit on and the items they will handle. Coordinating sound with the acting takes some consideration and time to integrate. When all of this is done, actors should be asked to wear their performance clothes, including shoes and whatever makeup the director and actors agree on.

Two techs and one dress rehearsal for a directing project may be sufficient, especially if the sound is simple. Large universities devote five or six full evenings of rehearsals to integrating all technical elements into the production and do two to three full dress rehearsals if the production is a complicated, multiset, period costume show. Coordinating lighting, sets, and music can be a time-consuming, meticulous process

FIGURE 5.33   Integrating the Technical Production. This scene from Shakespeare's *Much Ado About Nothing* offers challenges to all involved during early technical rehearsals. Some scenery flies and some is moved from side to side on tracks, the "eye" is lighted from behind, and there is music and choreography. The actors are wearing and carrying elaborate masks. During technical rehearsals, time must be set aside to resolve challenges so that scenes can be played fully and confidently.

TIP: Wardrobe and Props

■ Ask the actors to select shoes from their wardrobes that are consistent with the characters. Get the males out of flip-flops and into loafers or oxfords if they are appropriate to the character. The women must relinquish their platform clompers in favor of pumps or heels, as appropriate. The distraction of inflexible wooden clogs as they make contact with hard flooring is disconcerting.

■ Suggest that actors select appropriate clothing of their own to wear. If the char-acter is a businessperson, an actor dressed in jeans and a sweatshirt will not carry the authority that seems to be needed. Also ask this actor to wear a belt.

■ Don't spring surprises on the actors just before they are to perform. If they must eat or drink, for example, have the appropriate materials ready for use during several rehearsals before the performance.

calling for many stops and repeats to rerun specific cues so that they are seamlessly integrated into the fabric of the production.

Both beginning directors and experienced ones must allow sufficient rehearsal time to integrate the physical production with the acting. Because, of necessity, the focus during techs and dress is on the nonacting aspects of the production, the director must have the actors' work well prepared before these rehearsals begin.

Experiences

Calls

Divide the group into thirds. Working separately, have each group stage an imaginary curtain call. One group can stage a simple company call, while the second group devises a more complicated call—one with each actor coming out separately and then taking a company call. The third group can stage a tableau call in which the actors are frozen in a particularly strong picture, then have the actors break the tableau and take a company call positioned across the downstage area. Discuss the effectiveness of each call.

▄▄▄ KEY TERMS

With sufficient study of Step Five, you should be able to fully define the following terms:

- Actor-centered blocking
- Balance
- Blocking
- Body language
- Business
- Choice
- Collaborative blocking
- Composition
- Crossing
- Curtain call
- Director-centered blocking
- Elements of focus
- Flat and circle turns
- Goals of blocking
- Imperative verb phrases
- Indicating
- Intensifying the action
- Open/closed positions
- Pace
- Picturization

- Playable objectives
- Polishing
- Prompt script symbols
- Run-through goals
- Shape
- Side-coaching
- Solidity
- Stage area values
- Staging
- Strong and weak stage area
- Strong movements
- Table work
- Taking and giving stage
- Tempo
- Three-quarters open and closed
- UR, DL, and so on
- Weak movements

▓▓ WEB CONNECTIONS FOR MORE . . .

These Web sites will help you understand more about Rehearsing.

- Using a search engine like Google, download a free calendar planning program from the Web. You will be able to plan productions with the large calendar pages that are usually included in such programs.
- Using a search engine, separately enter the following terms: "theatre rehearsal," "rehearsal schedules," and "rehearsal process." Browse through the available hits to learn more about rehearsing, especially how other directors and theatres schedule and manage them.

STEP

6

Giving and Receiving Criticism

Theatre art can contain and express anything in the world and create worlds never seen before. This fact is one reason a director is never finished learning the art. Every production engenders responses, whether the director is aware of them or not. Much critical response is worthless, but some is priceless. One important way to grow is to listen seriously and thoughtfully to the feedback your production generates.

▬ OVERVIEW

Directors, no matter what their level of experience, must realize that a theatre performance is not really over until some audience and production members have shared their various reactions to the performance. Sometimes they chat directly to the director; sometimes the director hears secondhand comments. This aspect of the directing process can be a mixed blessing to fragile egos. Feedback, however, allows the director to grow by completing the circle of communication. The dedicated director not only listens but hears what is being said.

There are two sources of feedback, however, that the director must absolutely *hear:* the audience response in the theatre during a performance and the director's own instinct. Audiences seldom lie; their reactions can be ones of amazement, laughter appropriate or unwelcome, indifference, or outright hostility. Directors must listen to what the audience is telling them, process the reactions, and learn from it. Of course, the director must also listen to the artist within to discover the strengths and weaknesses of the production. If the director can raise the volume of this inner voice, it will give valuable information, especially after the performance has faded from immediate memory.

▬ GOALS

When you have read and studied this chapter, you should be able to do the following:

- Understand why compliments are rewarding to hear but that real directorial growth comes from hearing what, in your work, needs additional attention

- Use the Receiving Criticism checklist to guide your behavior during feedback sessions
- Initiate a feedback session with grace
- Follow the Receiving Criticism checklist when giving production responses to classmates

■ AN OPPORTUNITY TO LEARN

Everyone who has seen the production will have an opinion and many will want to express it. Some respondents will love the work and others may be quite negative. The best overall advice is to pay the most attention to the unflattering responses. If some responses must be ignored, let them be the global, affirming assessments. "It was great! I loved it!" is reassuring, but what can the director learn from this response? Respondents who try to be unduly supportive and nurturing mean well, but they may prevent the director from coming to grips with shortcomings and thus impede directorial growth. Criticism must be understood and heeded if the director is to grow as an artist.

Not all feedback, however, is helpful or painless to hear or read. Criticism is a form of self-expression that reflects only the individual making the observation, so it should be processed by the director with this understanding in mind. Some critics are worth noting; others can be dismissed. So, to whom does the beginning director turn for helpful responses? Listen to the responses given by those you respect, a mentor, or a significant other. And, yes, your instructor!

Most instructors view production miscalculations as "teaching moments" to be directed at the entire class. They may quite quickly and efficiently list what was

TIP: Getting Started with Feedback

An effective way to begin a feedback session is to ask each director of the project being discussed to state what they would do if they had three more rehearsals: How would the director use the extra rehearsal time?

This open-ended question breaks the ice by letting the director begin the feedback process with the tacit admission that not all aspects of the performance were perfect. The discussion leader, usually the instructor, can then invite comments from the group by asking first what aspects of the production were strong, then move to investigating what about the production needed more attention.

Specific areas of discussion might include:

- The project's general level of preparedness
- Quality and effectiveness of the acting, given the casting pool
- Composition and picturization
- Business
- Body language
- Ground plan effectiveness
- Management of the production's shape

successful in your work and then focus on a problem in blocking, for example, to reteach some strategies of picturization to the class. It may seem that an inordinate amount of time is spent emphasizing what didn't work in your production. You might want to consider a private conference with the instructor to discuss specific aspects of your directing work. This way you can get a balanced response at a time when you are more relaxed and able to learn from it.

Receiving Criticism

When feedback is offered by an instructor and classmates, here are some strategies for understanding what is being said, profiting from the analysis offered, and managing your response. The following five guidelines for accepting criticism can lead to making you a better director:

- *Tuck your ego in your back pocket.* Learn from your miscalculations. The purpose of the critique is to help you identify shortcomings so that you can improve on the next directing project. Criticism doesn't necessarily have to be about the director's miscalculations. The best critique might be the opening of other avenues of pursuit: "What if you'd done it this way instead?" You can grow as an artist only if you are serious about improving your skills.
- *Listen.* Don't be defensive. Don't argue. Be quiet! *Hear* what is being said.
- *Take notes.* Make notes about what is being said and why. Write it down so that you can study the comments in tranquility. The process of writing will calm the mind and aid memory, even if you never look at the notes again.
- *Ask questions.* It is helpful to ask, "I'm not clear on what you mean by . . . " if you don't understand what is being said. Don't defend yourself. A director must bypass rationalizations when receiving feedback. Of course, the production would have been more effective with better actors, with controlled lighting, a less-challenging script, or more production values—everyone knows that.
- *Assess.* Sometime you will hear contradictory responses. If one person thought your ground plan was effective but another thought it was flawed, then your job is to ferret out what is really being said by mulling over the specifics of the various comments and drawing your own (perhaps, quite different) conclusion. Perhaps both respondents were really talking about the blocking! Assessing responses to your work is best done in private and at a later time.

Giving Criticism

Just as you received responses from your classmates and instructor, you will be expected to comment on other class projects. Make sure your comments are about specific responses to directorial choices rather than your summary judgment. When you give feedback to fellow classmates, consider the following approaches:

- *Be direct.* If you don't understand a directional choice for the production, say so. Don't back into the response by starting with, "I was really excited by your production! It was wonderful! But . . . "
- *Be specific.* Don't give global evaluations. Avoid words like "good" and "bad." Ground your response in specifics and use the terminology found in this book. Instead of volunteering, "I liked the production until the last moments," a more helpful response would be, "I couldn't tell when the climax was."
- *Ask questions.* Find out what the director had in mind by asking why certain choices were made. "Why did you have Martha do . . . " is much preferable to "I didn't like it when Martha did . . . "
- *Be honest.* Don't flatter when it is not warranted. It's better to note that you thought the ground plan inhibited movement by asking, "How did you settle on the ground plan? I felt it needed to have another place for the actors to sit."
- *Be kind.* Focus on the production you have just seen rather than the personalities involved. Say, "I felt the production was quite successful. I enjoyed watching these actors" if you are being honest. If you can't honestly say this, you might consider commenting, "To me, Barbara didn't seem well cast in this part."
- *Respond to successful aspects.* Give feedback on all production aspects if possible, especially those that were the most successful. However, don't invent aspects to compliment if such feedback was not earned.

Experiences

Criticism

As a group, discuss the nature of artistic criticism. Do you (does the class) endorse the advice given in this final step of the directing process? Why? Why not?

EPILOGUE

Thinking Back and Looking Forward

You are no longer a beginning director! You've guided a number of projects to fruition, and in so doing, cast and managed the production process, received feedback from your colleagues and instructor, worked with a variety of actors, and explored a way to analyze a playscript. Clearly, you now have training and experience. What's the next step?

First, some questions that may bring your experiences into sharper focus. There are no right or wrong answers to these questions, there is only private contemplation.

- *Did you enjoy the experience?* If not, perhaps directing is not for you.
- *Did the projects you directed come alive?* Why did that happen? Why not? Was it due mainly to the actors you cast? Or, do you believe you guided them to give energized and clear performances?
- *What is your evaluation of the directing process?* What do you believe you did well? What did you do least well? Why? The answers to these questions will begin to help you define your directorial strategy.
- *Did you grow as an artist?* In what ways? Was your growth mainly as a craftsperson? Think about this issue because it will help you set future directing goals.
- *What aspects of your craft need to be improved?* Make a list, in descending order of importance, of specific areas of directing that need improvement. Read more about those areas in other directing texts. Perhaps this experience will give you a better insight into the problems and how they might be solved.
- *Was there one particularly illuminating experience?* Deliberate on the revelation. Can you describe it? How can you build on it? Can you repeat it?
- *Do you believe your actors trusted you?* If not, why? Try to isolate your directorial qualities that elicited confidence, or caused them to doubt you. Should you seek further training as an actor in order to be a better director of actors?
- *Are you ready to work with designers?* Why? Why not? Perhaps further training in stage and/or lighting design will illuminate the design process and give you more confidence.

The answers to these and other questions will help you discover where you stand in the director's "lifelong journey." Private reflection can lead to growth. Perhaps you can discuss some of the issues here with a mentor who might then be able to confirm some of your conclusions.

KEEP DIRECTING

This first part of the beginning director's journey was devoted to short playscripts and/or scenes from full-length plays. You should now be ready to face the challenges of long one-act plays (thirty minutes or more) and/or long plays. Finding a venue to direct in may be difficult but the following suggestions may prove helpful.

Classroom Venues

Approach the instructor of an introduction to theatre course and volunteer to produce and direct a long scene for that class. Ask for suggestions of material that would facilitate the teaching of the course. Then do it! Or you might approach the teacher of a dramatic literature course and make the same offer. If there is a playwriting course, ask to work with one of the students in that class and then direct a scene or short play.

High School Programs

Secondary schools often produce one or two playscripts a year. Contact the teacher in charge of the theatre program to discover if there is a slot for you as an assistant director. After successful completion of this assignment, again approach the teacher about directing the next production.

Civic Theatres

Community theatres sometimes program an evening of short plays as part of their season. Ask how you might go about applying for a directing slot. Perhaps you can invite a member of the theatre's play selection committee to see your directing work at one of the venues just suggested. Again, you could volunteer to be an assistant director to one of their experienced directors.

MORE SUGGESTIONS

In addition to gaining more directing experience, the director who is dedicated to making the journey will look for other experiences. Expanding your knowledge of theatre on stage and on the page may be at the heart of further growth.

See Theatre Performances

See all sorts of plays directed from various viewpoints. See community and educational theatre productions, but make a special effort to attend professional presentations by significant not-for-profit theatres. See Broadway and Off-Broadway productions. Touring shows should be part of the mix too. The main goal is to discover how others practice the art and craft of directing. Some approaches will not attract you, while others will surprise and charm you. The point is to experience a broad range of live theatre in commercial, not-for-profit, educational, and amateur venues.

If a production is lackluster, consider what you could have done to improve it. If a production is first-rate, consider going to it a second time; with the surprise of seeing the first performance behind you, the work of the director, designers, and actors should become clearer.

Read Plays and Memoirs

Set a goal of reading at least fifteen to twenty plays a year for your own enjoyment and edification. Some should be new playscripts, others can be modern classics, and still others should come from the rest of the world's dramatic literature. This text has drawn examples from several playscripts. Do you know them? If not, you might begin by reading the scripts mentioned here.

Diaries and memoirs published by important directors, actors, and designers will offer insight on some of the issues facing you. Some choices for additional reading follow.

Keep a Journal

When you see a production that intrigues you, note the title and author in a journal along with a few of the qualities that attracted you. Were you fascinated by the production strategy or the literature? When you read and like a playscript, note that too, and then list its admirable qualities. This journal may prove useful if you are ever invited to suggest a playscript you would like to direct.

A journal is an appropriate place to make notes about your additional reading and also observations about the directing process based on theatre productions you see.

TIP: Ushering

Volunteer as an usher. It's a cheap way to see many productions. Roadhouses, community theatres, local not-for-profits, and educational theatres always need ushers. There are often signup sheets, so all it takes is finding out where and how to sign up.

Even in large metropolitian areas, such as New York City and Boston, ushers are recruited in return for the chance to see the production free. Go to *www.playbill.com* and click on the Jobs link. There may be usher postings that correspond to a time you can be in New York.

Further Coursework

Is there a more advanced directing course you can take? Another course could introduce you to a new textbook with a fuller, more complete exploration of the directing process. You could continue probing the art and craft of directing under nurturing conditions, perhaps culminating in your first directorial public performance.

■ ADDITIONAL READING

Bartow, Arthur. *The Director's Voice: Twenty-One Interviews.*

Bogart, Anne. *A Director Prepares: Seven Essays on Art and Theatre.*

Brook, Peter. *The Empty Space.*

Clurman, Harold. *On Directing.*

Cole, Toby, and Chinoy, Helen Kirch, Eds. *Directors on Directing: A Source Book for the Modern Theater,* Revised Edition.

Cole, Susan Letzler. *Directors in Rehearsal: A Hidden World.*

Daniels, Rebecca. *Women Stage Directors Speak.*

Guthrie, Tyrone. *A Life in the Theater: Tyrone Guthrie on Acting.*

Hodge, Francis. *Play Directing: Analysis, Communication, and Style,* Fifth Edition.

Houghton, Norris. *Moscow Rehearsals.*

Kazan, Elia. *Elia Kazan: A Life.*

Krasner, David, Ed. *Method Acting Reconsidered: Theory, Practice, Future.*

Styan, J. L. *Max Reinhardt.*

Thomas, James. *Script Analysis for Actors, Directors, and Designers,* Second Edition.

APPENDIXES

Appendixes A and B each contain ten-minute plays that can be used as a basis for the experiences found throughout this book. These plays, along with nine others, were given a staged reading by Primary Stages Company in New York on March 7, 2002, under the collective title of "A Moment of Bliss." Tyler Marchant, associate artistic director of the Primary Stages Company, was the event's curator.

Mae and Her Stories was fully staged by the Cafe Theatre at George Street Playhouse, New Brunswick, New Jersey, in a production directed by Andrea Arden with Terri Sturtevant as Mae, Justin Romeo as Shawn, and Catlin Mulhern as Beth. David Hoffman was the producer. Performance rights to *Mae and Her Stories* are available by writing the author: David DeWitt, 50 West 72nd Street, #604, New York, NY 10023.

Cha-Cha-Cha was fully staged by Native Aliens at the Flatiron Playhouse in New York City. Jodi Smith directed Melissa Wolff and Tony Schremmer. Performance rights to *Cha-Cha-Cha* are available by writing the author: Garth Wingfield, 455 West 23rd Street, #10A, New York, NY 10011.

Appendix C contains a brief history of the director in the modern and postmodern theatre. The director as we know it today did not emerge until the latter half of the nineteenth century, and was enhanced by the growing interest and fascination with the modern, realistic worldview that audiences demanded. This change, along with the development of acting methods, affected the production of a play in such a way that the creativity, ingenuity, and diversity of directors flourished.

APPENDIX A

Mae and Her Stories

BY DAVID DEWITT

Characters

- MAE, a pharmacy cashier in Charlotte, NC. Late 40s to early 60s. A warm, positive survivor.
- BETH, who also plays THE ACTRESS and THE MOTHER. Best played by an actress in her mid-20s.
- SHAWN, who also plays THE PRESS and THE FATHER. Best played by an actor in his mid-20s.

SETTING: Mae's den and worldview in Charlotte, NC.

AT RISE: MAE is on a couch, covered with layers of blankets, with a cup of tea. She is watching Shawn and Beth.

SHAWN: We should run away.

BETH: I can't run away.

SHAWN: You have to stop saying "I can't."

BETH: Shawn.

SHAWN: *(mocking)* "I can't go to the city."

BETH: I don't—

SHAWN: "I can't stay out after dark."

BETH: Stop—

SHAWN: "I can't—"

BETH: Stop it!

SHAWN: "I can't do anything myself!"

BETH: Don't tease me. I have enough problems. Just please don't tease me.

SHAWN: OK. *(a beat)* Beth? I was serious.

BETH: About what?

SHAWN: That we could run away.

(He touches BETH. MAE points to them as if pausing them with a television remote control; they freeze for a moment, though they will relax and move at some point as MAE speaks to the audience.)

MAE: I watch television. I watch it a lot. And I don't get all you people who say there's never anything good on TV. How would you know if you never look? I'm not talking about the news shows, the MSNBC, the CNN, CNBC, the E, the, I don't know, all those new alphabet channels. They muddle up your head just thinking about them. News. I can't watch the news. Too much information. I watch the programs, my stories. I remember my grandmama, whatever she had to do, and she had a lot to do, her day would stop in its tracks for her stories. Then all day long she'd be thinkin' 'bout Alice and Steve and whoever else while she was ironing another blouse for my mama. Nowadays we've got so much TV you'd have to be a rock not to find a story you like—as long as you're willing to look. Me, I found this one show called *Southern Crosses*. It's on—well, it's on Channel 9 where I am, but you'll have to look it up where you are. Because it's different, you know, depending on where you are. *(SHAWN is now THE FATHER of BETH.)* It's about this preacher and his family in this small town.

BETH: Why can't I go?

THE FATHER: What did your mother say?

BETH: She says I can't go.

THE FATHER: Then you don't need to ask me.

BETH: But she said I could ask you.

THE FATHER: Did she? Elizabeth Marie? Don't lie to me.

BETH: I'm not lying, Daddy.

THE FATHER: Because if you're not telling the truth, it will come out.

BETH: Oh, sure it will.

THE FATHER: What did you say?

BETH: Can I go? Please?

THE FATHER: Is there a chaperone?

BETH: Daddy, I'm seventeen.

THE FATHER: That's right, you're seventeen, and that's too young to go out of town without a chaperone.

BETH: All the other kids do it.

THE FATHER: You aren't all the other kids. You're part of this family and more importantly you're part of the family of God. You're not going on the trip, Elizabeth Marie. That's final.

BETH: That's not fair.

THE FATHER: When you're older, you'll understand.

MAE: No, she won't.

THE FATHER: I have to finish my sermon. *(a beat)* Is there something else?

BETH: No, there's nothing else.

MAE: I have a feeling about this girl who plays the preacher's daughter. She's really good, true to life, and she's got a really good story right now. I heard the girl who plays her do this interview once?

(BETH becomes THE ACTRESS; SHAWN becomes THE PRESS.)

THE ACTRESS: She's going to have a strong arc this season and become much more mature. She's not going to accept everything she's been taught. You could say she's becoming a woman.

THE PRESS: And with the hunky Joshua Lee Hanson as her boyfriend, can we expect that she'll finally have sex?

THE ACTRESS: Well, it's about time, isn't it? I mean, she's already seventeen! But you'll have to tune in to find out. I can tell you that whatever happens, you can bet you'll be surprised.

(MAE pauses them; they freeze.)

MAE: The show's not as bad as that sounds. *(Beth and Shawn again; they begin to kiss.)* I can't stop watching it. For the life of me, I can't stop watching it.

BETH: I can't—

SHAWN: Yes, you can. Who cares what they say? We'll go anyhow.

BETH: My mama would kill me.

SHAWN: Your folks are going to ruin your life.

BETH: What do you want me to do?

SHAWN: I was thinking about that. You trust me, right? *(BETH nods. SHAWN kneels.)* Let's run away. Let's leave town forever. I mean it, let's just go, right now.

BETH: Shawn. I can't.

SHAWN: "I can't, I can't." Beth. I love you. When are you going to start saying "I can"? Your folks can't tell you how to live. They don't care anyway, not really. And I love you.

BETH: I love you too. *(She kneels with him.)*

SHAWN: I know. *(He moves to kiss her.)*

MAE: When I saw what they were doing—

BETH: Oh, Shawn—*(BETH and SHAWN kiss.)*

MAE: I thought I was going to die. *(BETH and SHAWN freeze.)* It's the strangest thing. Maybe because the preacher sort of reminds me of my daddy. He wasn't a preacher, my daddy; he was a banker.

(BETH becomes THE MOTHER.)

THE MOTHER: Elizabeth Marie!

MAE: And my mama was—this woman—

THE MOTHER: Elizabeth Marie. Did you go to your father behind my back? Don't you turn your head, don't you do it! You aren't too old for me to give you a good spankin'! Don't you forget that!

MAE: She won't.

THE MOTHER: I don't know what's got into you. I just don't know. But I think I've decided it's this boy—be quiet! I think it's this boy you've been seein'. He's fillin' your head with somethin', I don't know what. Now I've thought about this, and I've prayed about this, and the only thing I can think to do is tell you that you can't see him anymore. That's it, that's my decision, so don't you talk back to me and don't you run to your father. He has work to do, Work with a capital W. All right, that's—honey? Don't waste those tears on me, I know better. Now go on. Go on now. *(As if the daughter has left and she's calling her back.)* Beth? These boys, they won't matter in a few years. I promise you that.

MAE: I could just hear my mama saying that. *(THE MOTHER turns away. She will become BETH again, with SHAWN.)* Talk about hooked. I started recording every episode of *Southern Crosses,* and sometimes I'd have marathons on the weekend. Here's what I do. I make myself a cup of Perfect Peach tea and cuddle up with some blankets and sit right here and watch the TV all alone for hours and hours and hours and . . . You think I'm sort of pitiful, don't you? "That poor woman, watching television instead of living her life."

SHAWN: *(to BETH)* You've got to live your own life.

MAE: That's right. And I do. I'm a cashier in a drugstore. Super X. That's with the "r" and the "x" hooked like a prescription, you know. But Super. I'm a Super Cashier. I like it. I guess it might sound boring, but see, it all depends on how you look at it. If you're like my daddy the banker, you might not think much of my job; but Daddy, he was all about Work with a capital W. At the drugstore, I'm all about life with a capital L-I-F-E. You know why? Every day I get to see what it takes to keep a life going. One customer takes something for blood pressure, another one takes something for cholesterol. He's taking a sleeping pill, she's taking insulin. Just about everyone has something, something that's gone wrong, it's part of life. It's pretty amazing. And sometimes they get better. Think about that. And I get to watch. *(SHAWN moves to embrace BETH.)* I like getting to watch that. Just like I like getting to watch *Southern Crosses.*

(BETH pushes SHAWN away.)

SHAWN: What's wrong?

BETH: Can we just talk?

SHAWN: You talk too much.

BETH: But I—

SHAWN: Beth—you get to the point where you have to do something. You're almost eighteen. We can do something.

BETH: Are you—are you talking about—*(SHAWN kisses her.)*

SHAWN: Yeah. *(SHAWN kisses BETH more intensely; she squirms.)*

BETH: I can't—

SHAWN: It's OK.

BETH: No—

SHAWN: It's OK. I love you.

BETH: No—

SHAWN: I said it's OK! *(SHAWN pushes BETH to the ground, lies on top of her.)* There. *(a beat)* It's OK.

BETH: I can't.

SHAWN: Relax. *(He touches her breast.)*

BETH: No.

SHAWN: Beth—

BETH: No!

SHAWN: Shut up! *(He puts his hand over her mouth. She makes a sound and begins to cry. He begins to grind against her.)* Shhhh. It's OK. Shhhh. Just shhhhh.

MAE: He's a son of a bitch. I can't believe what I'm seeing. What I'm saying. He's a son of a bitch.

(BETH rises; she has been raped and should somehow look it.)

BETH: Daddy! *(SHAWN gets up and walks past Mae. He will stroke her hair as he passes; MAE will react.)* Daddy! Daddy, are you here? Daddy!

(SHAWN has become THE FATHER.)

THE FATHER: Elizabeth Marie. This is a church.

MAE: For me, it was the bank.

THE FATHER: Elizabeth Marie. This is a bank.

BETH: But Daddy—

THE FATHER: Shhhh! Before anything else, just shhhh! Now what is it?

BETH AND MAE: Something happened.

THE FATHER: Is this about the argument you had with your mother?

BETH: No—

THE FATHER: Because I have told you again and again not to come to me about disagreements with your mother. You've got to grow up about these things. You're seventeen. You work this out.

BETH: I can't.

THE FATHER: And this boy you're seeing?

BETH: He—

THE FATHER: Your mother doesn't think he's a good influence, and I have to agree. You're a member of this family and the family of God. You can't just go with him on an out-of-town trip. You can't just do whatever you want. Don't cry. You can't go.

BETH: Daddy!

THE FATHER: Shhh! This is a bank.

BETH: That's not—

THE FATHER: The subject is closed. I'll see you tonight. *(BETH moves to leave, stops.)* What?

BETH AND MAE: Bye, Daddy.

THE FATHER: I'll see you tonight. *(BETH walks to MAE. MAE opens her arms. BETH sits with MAE, who wraps her in a blanket.)*

MAE: The father doesn't see her that night. Beth runs off and becomes a model in New York City. I just ran off and became a cashier in Charlotte *(considers BETH; a beat).* She's so good, this girl. I'm so glad I found her. *(BETH stands, folds a blanket.)* I've seen lots of stories. I've loved lots of stories. But I never thought I would see my story, that other people would care about my story. You know? *(BETH offers her hand to MAE. MAE stands and they embrace.)* But—I think it's a good story.

THE FATHER: Elizabeth Marie, I'm so sorry. *(BETH and MAE break their embrace. BETH leaves.)*

MAE: This is what I wish would happen. *(to the FATHER)* Daddy? Do you humbly repent your sins?

THE FATHER: Whatever you say.

MAE: *(to the audience)* I love that.

THE FATHER: Thank God the truth came out. I should have listened to you.

THE MOTHER: I'm sorry too.

MAE: You should be, Mother.

THE MOTHER: And Elizabeth Marie? I was wrong when I said you'd forget that boy. I didn't know.

MAE: You didn't know squat.

THE MOTHER: Whatever you say. I didn't know squat.

SHAWN: Beth?

MAE: *(to the audience)* Him.

SHAWN: I didn't know anything either. I was wrong. I thought I loved you, and I just wanted you to love me.

MAE: Here's the best thing about the stories. In life, I wouldn't speak to him. But on TV? *(to SHAWN)* You're out of the show. You'll be hit by a mack truck.

SHAWN: Whatever you say.

THE ACTRESS: Beth is the best character I've ever played. I love her. I'm not just saying that. I'm so lucky I found her. I feel she's made me a more healthy human being.

MAE: I do too. *(Mae moves back to her seat.)* Nowadays I find a lot of stories that I love. I sort of think it's my talent. I find lots of things that hit me like the *Crosses.*

THE PRESS: But won't you tell the viewing audience why this is your favorite story?

(He indicates a "microphone" turned to MAE. She reacts, then says to the THE PRESS and the audience:)

MAE: I would tell the viewing audience that they would be surprised at how many favorite stories I can have. I keep finding 'em. Because I look. If you look, you'll find something you like. Just look at me.

(End of play.)

Cha-Cha-Cha

BY GARTH WINGFIELD

Characters

- HENRY, late thirties. He is good looking. Snappily dressed.
- SHEILA, late thirties. Attractive, much more so than she realizes. Nicely dressed.

SETTING: A crowded party. SHEILA stands alone, sipping wine and smiling faintly as an early 80s song plays. After a moment, HENRY approaches. He's wearing a suit and tie.

HENRY: *(cautious)* Sheila . . . ?

SHEILA: *(turns, caught off guard)* I'm sorry?

HENRY: You're Sheila, right?

SHEILA: I am . . .

HENRY: *(sort of overwhelmed)* Wow . . . okay, this is . . . It's Henry.

SHEILA: Oh . . . oh, okay, sure—oh my God, hi!

HENRY: Henry Glassman.

SHEILA: Yes, of course!

HENRY: It's so wonderful to see you.

SHEILA: Sure, you too!

HENRY: I was over there by the cash-bar getting a drink, and I saw you and thought: Wait, that's Sheila Coogan. Jesus! And I just . . . I figured I'd come over and say hello. So . . . hello.

SHEILA: Hello!

HENRY: Can I get you . . . do you want a wine or anything?

SHEILA: No, I'm all set.

HENRY: You sure?

SHEILA: Yeah.

HENRY: Man, this is . . .

SHEILA: I know!

HENRY: I'm just . . . I don't know what to . . . ahhh! *(Collects himself a little, then:)* How are you?

SHEILA: I'm well, thanks.

HENRY: That's great. So great. I'm really pleased to hear that.

(A beat.)

HENRY: You have no idea who I am, do you?

SHEILA: I don't!

HENRY: I had a feeling . . .

SHEILA: *(looks at his name tag)* Henry Glassman . . .

HENRY: Well, I was Hank back in school.

SHEILA: Okay . . .

HENRY: Hank Glassman.

SHEILA: That sounds a bit more familiar . . .

HENRY: Um, let me . . . I was on the debate team in ninth grade . . .

SHEILA: Uh-huh . . .

HENRY: I was friends with your brother Kendall for about five minutes in *tenth* grade . . .

SHEILA: Okay . . .

HENRY: I think we were in Mrs. Lyons' AP English class senior year . . .

SHEILA: *(realizes)* Oh my God, you used to be fat!

(A little beat.)

HENRY: *(smiles awkwardly)* I . . . did . . .

SHEILA: You used to be so fat!

HENRY: I wouldn't go that far . . .

SHEILA: I remember now . . . vaguely . . . you were . . . real tubby there for a few years. You wore Husky pants from Sears. You had breasts.

HENRY: You're crossing a line now, Sheila . . .

SHEILA: And now here you are. My God, look at you! This is chubby little Hank Glassman. You're in such great shape now—you must be gay!

(A little beat.)

HENRY: Excuse me?

SHEILA: I'm sorry, that was the wine talking—I shouldn't have had this last glass. It's just . . . you're so svelte now. And defined!

HENRY: *(awkward)* I don't know about that . . .

SHEILA: Please, look around this room. You're toned. It's very clear that the men in our class have completely forgotten the meaning of the word "gym."

HENRY: Okay . . . *(looks at her name tag)* So it's Sheila *Hennessee* now . . .

SHEILA: It is. That's my husband over there, Ted. He's in real estate. And we've got two kids. Charlie, six; Joe, three.

HENRY: How wonderful . . . *(Then:)* And what about you?

SHEILA: What about me?

HENRY: Well, what do you do?

SHEILA: *(a little taken aback)* Oh . . . well, I don't know . . . I carpool. I garden. I volunteer at the women's center. *(Then:)* I paint, but we don't talk about that.

HENRY: *(smiles, pressing)* Why don't we?

SHEILA: Because it's . . . *nothing*, it's . . .

HENRY: Like acrylics? Watercolors, or . . . ?

SHEILA: *(plows ahead)* But no, no—tell me more about *you,* Henry Glassman! What are you up to these days?

HENRY: How do you mean?

SHEILA: What's your life like? What's happened to you? I'm so curious to find out!

HENRY: Well . . . you know . . . I'm gay.

SHEILA: *(after a little beat)* I'm sorry?

HENRY: I live in New York. I'm an architect. I go to a great gym in Chelsea and eat mostly low-fat.

I just broke up with this guy I've been seeing for seven years—messy breakup, we lived together, awful, awful. He cheated; there were cats involved. I hope I'm not shocking you.

SHEILA: *(forced smile)* No! No, not at all. At *all*!

HENRY: All thing's considered, I'm doing okay. *(a beat)* So, um . . . how much do you actually remember about me?

SHEILA: You know . . . this and that. I'll admit I'm sort of iffy . . .

HENRY: Because I remember you quite well.

SHEILA: You do?

HENRY: Sure.

SHEILA: Me? Oh, come on . . .

HENRY: Please, you were one of the great beauties of our class!

SHEILA: *(wry)* "Were." Exactly. Not anymore . . .

HENRY: What are you talking about? You look great!

SHEILA: I've had two kids. It shows.

HENRY: *(ignores that)* I remember in tenth grade you were a cheerleader, and at this one pep rally—it was against St. Stephen's, I think—you shouted so much you got hoarse, but you kept at it anyway, barking out the cheers like a seal. You were adorable . . .

SHEILA: Really? That happened? That was *ages* ago . . .

HENRY: And also I remember you wore fishnet hose to school one day for no reason whatsoever. Very racy.

SHEILA: *(stunned at that)* Oh my God . . . !

HENRY: And then, well, you were Bloody Mary in *South Pacific.* Ridiculous casting, but you made it work.

SHEILA: I can't believe you remember *that* . . . !

HENRY: Of course I do! I'm sure everyone does.

(A little beat.)

SHEILA: I'm so sorry, Henry. I wish I remembered you better.

HENRY: That's okay . . .

SHEILA: I have these hazy flashes . . . of you wearing very baggy clothes . . .

HENRY: It was a whole Mama Cass thing I was going for. Draping myself in muumuus and caftans . . . trying for this whole airy look . . . avoiding sandwiches . . .

SHEILA: *(giggles)* Oh, stop!

HENRY: Hey, it's understandable you barely remember me. I was a different person then.

SHEILA: You were. You really were.

(A beat.)

HENRY: May, um . . . may I make a huge confession here?

SHEILA: *(a little uneasy)* Okay . . .

HENRY: You were the first girl I ever had a major crush on.

SHEILA: I was? Are you serious?

HENRY: Oh, yeah. In ninth grade. Writing your name in my notebook, fantasizing about you endlessly, the whole deal. I had this one fantasy where we'd move to Paris and live in this all-white distressed loft space decorated very tastefully, but spare—a very spare esthetic— with Eames Chairs and a Saarinen dining table, very clean lines, maybe a chenille throw. *(then)* You can see why it never would've worked out.

SHEILA: I'm . . . well, I'm flattered. Did you ever tell me this?

HENRY: God, no! Come on . . .

SHEILA: Why not?

HENRY: Because . . . I don't know, because I was this Husky-wearing nerd who watched too much *Star Trek* . . . and you were *Sheila Coogan,* for God's sake!

SHEILA: Oh, please . . .

HENRY: *(then, catches himself)* Okay, for the record . . . it's not like I'm your "number-one fan" here or anything. I haven't been making crazy photo albums with your tiny picture from the yearbook all these years or collecting strands of your hair.

SHEILA: I didn't think that . . .

HENRY: To be honest, the crush only lasted six months, if that. I was over you by late spring. *So* over you. And I haven't thought about any of this in forever. Until just now . . . Until I saw you.

SHEILA: Right, looking a gazillion years old . . .

HENRY: You look great. Just great . . .

(A little beat.)

SHEILA: You know . . . I think . . . I might actually remember one tiny thing about you, Henry Glassman.

HENRY: You do?

SHEILA: *(still vague)* Were we . . . did we take ballroom dancing class together during, like . . . sophomore year?

HENRY: *(tries to remember)* Okay . . . well . . . yeah, I think we did. God, ballroom dancing . . . I haven't thought about *that* in ages.

SHEILA: I remember thinking it was so stupid at the time . . .

HENRY: Well, it was completely stupid. Like, what, we were gonna grow up, go to cocktail parties and be asked to do the *minuet* at the drop of a glove?

SHEILA: Wait, and who was that couple who taught the class? Lance something . . .

HENRY: Right, Lance . . . what was it?

SHEILA: *(it snaps into place)* Lance Romance and his lovely wife, Bubbles!

HENRY: His last name wasn't *Romance* . . .

SHEILA: No, but we called him that! And she really *was* named Bubbles—literally. With the glass eye!

HENRY: *(remembering himself)* Oh my God! And it . . . right, it became entirely apparent to Lance and Bubbles that they were losing their audience midway through the semester . . . that we all were realizing how pointless this was . . .

SHEILA: So they changed their music!

HENRY: Just tossed out the Strauss waltzes . . .

SHEILA: And the stuffy Lawrence Welk stuff . . .

HENRY: And brought in all these new records, something Top 40 . . .

SHEILA: *(then, a revelation)* Oh my God, I am ninety-seven percent certain that you and I did the cha-cha to Gloria Gaynor's "I Will Survive" at some point that spring!

HENRY: *(then, stunned)* Oh my God, we did!

SHEILA: We absolutely did!

HENRY: I can't believe you remember that!

SHEILA: Well, it was insane . . .

HENRY: I can't believe I'd *forgotten* that . . .

SHEILA: *(sorta sings, playful)* "So go on, go—cha-cha-cha— walk out the door—cha-cha-cha . . . "

HENRY: *(laughs)* Oh my God . . . !

SHEILA: *(as she kinda cha-chas)* I think they also made us fox trot to Kool & The Gang's "Celebration," but don't quote me on that.

HENRY: *(laughs)* You're a terrific dancer . . .

SHEILA: Oh, stop, I'm not at all . . .

HENRY: *(laughing, realizing)* I did the disco-dance cha-cha with the first girl I ever had a crush on—GOD, HOW UTTERLY PERFECT IS THAT?!

(At once, she leans in and kisses him. He kisses her back. Everything shifts. Silence.)

SHEILA: I . . . should find my husband . . .

HENRY: Oh . . . oh, sure . . . right . . .

SHEILA: It's just . . . he's gonna . . .

HENRY: No, yeah . . . of course . . .

(A little beat.)

SHEILA: It was great seeing you again, Henry.

HENRY: Yeah. Yeah, it really was . . . *(He starts to go, then stops.)* Keep, um . . . keep painting.

SHEILA: What? *(Then:)* Oh . . . okay, thanks . . . Keep . . . eating low fat.

HENRY: You know, fingers crossed . . . So maybe I'll see you again in twenty more years.

SHEILA: Right . . . twenty more years . . .

(He goes.)

SHEILA: *(to herself)* Right . . .

(The crowd is louder. Another song is playing. She sways slightly to the music.)

The End

The Director in the Modern and Postmodern Theatre
A Brief History

Playwrights and actors have existed, off and on and in different forms, since ancient times. Stage directors, however, are a modern innovation. The stage director as an independent theatre artist came into prominence only during the last quarter of the nineteenth century. Previously, the duties now assigned to the director were performed, if at all, by the playwright, the leading actor, the company manager, or the stage manager. While theatre certainly prospered without a director, productions were not characterized by the kind of theatrical unity that audiences now expect.

Before the invention of the role of the stage director, productions were controlled either by the playwright or a dominant actor. Scenery and costumes were either proscribed by tradition or catch-as-catch-can. The director added another artist to the mix, one responsible for coordinating the impact of all the elements involved with a theatrical production—playscript, acting, music, setting, costuming, and lighting.

The historical precedents that led to the emergence of the director began with the ancient Greeks. Playwrights during the Greek classical era supervised the production of their plays. The playwright read the play to the actors, perhaps explained difficult passages, and assigned entrances and exits. The playwright, or someone he appointed, also staged the chorus, teaching them movements and supervising their speaking/singing. Aeschylus was particularly noted for the production of his plays. In the Hellenistic and Greco-Roman eras, revivals of Greek plays were probably conducted by retired actors who had themselves performed in them. This production tradition passed from generation to generation, including Roman writers like Plautus and Terrence.

In the late medieval period, when religious pageants were staged outdoors as civic events, a city often hired a *maître de jeu* (or a *master of the performance* or *master of play*) to organize the entire production, including the special effects. One such organizer, Jean Bouchet, was acknowledged as a superior stager of religious pageants, working in many venues in many countries.

It is clear that Shakespeare had a significant hand in the production of his plays at the Globe Theatre. The texts of a few of his plays give ample evidence of his beliefs about acting and play production. The "advice to the players" in *Hamlet* is a stunning example:

> Speak the speech, I pray you, as I pronounced it to you, trippingly on the tongue. But if you mouth it, as many of our players do, I had as lief the town crier spoke my lines. Nor do not saw the air too much with your hand. . . .

191

At least one of Moliere's plays also provides advice as to how things should and should not be done in theatre production. As his company's playwright, leading actor, and manager, Moliere staged the plays his troupe mounted.

Where playwrights did not control the staging of plays, the actor-manager took over, usually a star actor whose name alone would attract an audience. The actor-manager booked a theatre, assembled a company of actors and technicians, and produced plays. The tradition of the actor-manager as supervisor of production throughout Europe is a long one. For example, David Garrick, in 1765 in London, would tell the actors of his company where to enter, where to stand, and where to exit. Rehearsals were very limited. Actors provided their own clothes, often the most expensive and fashionable they could afford, no matter what role they played. Actor-managers would instruct the stage manager to pull from the theatre's stock of generic scenic wings and backdrops those units that might be appropriate for the play.

If scenery were to be newly created for a production, the actor-manager would commission a painter to create drops that furnished a general background for the actors, often with little regard to the specific places mentioned in the play. Interiors were most often "royal" or "domestic." Exteriors were "pastoral" or "urban." While the resulting scenery might have provided a fetching *background*, the scenery by no means attempted to create the *environment* implied by the script.

The modern, realistic worldview that began to emerge and gain importance in the theatre after 1875 led audiences to eventually demand that what they saw on stage echo life as they understood and experienced it. That is, the production was required to reflect what the audience knew to be real. Reality, or truth, consisted of what could be verified by the senses: sight, sound, smell, touch, taste. The implication of this profound change in the standards of theatrical truth manifested itself in every aspect of theatrical production.

THE MODERN DIRECTOR

This realistic worldview greatly affected the physical production of a play. Sets had to mirror the specific given circumstances established by the text. The actors' costumes, their props, the furniture they used, and the way they behaved all had to reinforce the text. In short, audiences for the first time expected a production that was *unified*, one that reflected their own understanding not only of the physical world but of the psychological behavior of the playwright's characters. Audiences wanted to see bravura acting but expected all of the company to support the central actors in a unified production.

The person responsible for unifying the production in this way was a new theatre artist called the director. The first modern director, an independent theatre artist, is acknowledged to be George II, Duke of Saxe-Meiningen. George II supervised his small, private court theatre company to produce innovative ensemble productions, characterized by historically accurate sets, costumes, makeup, and props. Unlike the standard stage practice of the time, his productions were meticulously rehearsed, including intricately staged crowd scenes that became the company's hallmark.

Through his leadership and vision, and with the help of Ludwig Chronegk (stage manager) and Ellen Franz (lead actress and coach), the Duke of Saxe-Meiningen is regarded as the first modern theatre director. Word of the extraordinary Meiningen Players soon garnered them invitations to play all over Europe. They toured from 1874 to 1890, presenting well over 2,000 performances in 36 cities in Europe and Russia.

The Meiningen company was seen by and strongly influenced the next generation of theatre artists in Europe, including Henry Irving in London, Andre Antoine in France, and Otto Braham and Max Reinhardt in Germany. The Meiningen productions made a lasting impression on the Russian theatre artist, Constantin Stanislavski.

The Theatre Duke: George II, Duke of Saxe-Meiningen (1826–1914)

In 1866, George II came to the throne of a small duchy in what is now Germany. Almost immediately he revitalized his court theatre by enlisting the help of an actor, Ludwig Chronegk (1837–1891), whom George II named manager of the acting company. It was Chronegk who planned the tours that made the Meiningen Players famous. George II himself took an active part in organizing and designing the theatre's productions. Another important leader of the company was the actress Ellen Franz (1839–1923), whom George II married in 1873. Franz was responsible for coaching the actors' stage speech and selecting and editing the repertory.

George II, who had extensive art training, designed all of the sets, costumes, and properties, guided by extensive period research. The result was historically accurate productions that were unparalleled when compared to other theatre companies of that time. The use of authentic and expensive materials for props, settings, and especially costume fabrics characterized the duke's productions. Three-dimensional scenery was another hallmark of the Meiningen Players. The use of platforms, dimensional set pieces, steps, and stairs all created an environment rather than a background. For the first time the dimensionality of the scenery matched the dimensionality of the actor.

The Meiningen Players did not feature stars. The duke's small acting company functioned as a well-rehearsed ensemble. All the actors, including the leading players, were made a part of the crowd if they were not otherwise cast. Rehearsals were long and intense and the play was not scheduled for performance until it was deemed ready by George II, Chronegk, and Franz. The productions that toured England, Germany, Sweden, Austria, Denmark, Holland, and Russia changed the face of theatre in Europe.

■ A NEW WAY TO ACT

Constantin Stanislavski (1865–1938) expanded the Duke of Saxe-Meiningen's directing methods by developing a way to act that embraced the emerging realistic worldview. Working with the actors of the Moscow Art Theatre, which he cofounded in 1898, Stanislavski devised an acting process that mined the psychological, physical, and emotional truth of character. Four books published between 1924 and 1961 set forth his views on theatre—especially acting—and exerted tremendous influence on the training of subsequent generations of actors in Europe and America.

The Stanislavski system has a dozen or so tenets that still form the basis of most actor training in the United States. Knowing and understanding this approach to acting will help the new director communicate with actors. The beginning director should be familiar with the following acting precepts:

- *Finding and playing character objectives:* Discovering what the character wants during the entire arc of the play (called the *superobjective*) and what the character wants at every specific moment (called the *objective*)
- *Discovering and playing units of action:* Breaking the play into action units
- *Mapping the play's given circumstances:* Discovering the *who, what, where,* and *when* as supplied by the playwright
- *Playing active verbs:* Playing the *why,* the character's motivation
- *Playing the subtext:* Communicating what the character really means
- *Personalization and the magic if:* Using the question "What would I do if I were in these circumstances?"
- *Relaxation:* The release of actor tension so that the body can accept and act on the character's stimuli
- *Employing affective memory:* Incorporating emotional memory ("how I felt then") and sense memory ("my physical reaction to the five senses") into the actor's characterization
- *The technique of substitution:* Asking, "How can I use experiences from my life to enrich the character's life?"
- *Distilling concentration:* Narrowing the circle of concentration to what is happening to the character in the here and now
- *Valuing the ensemble:* Making sure each actor is telling the same story in the same style

The visit of the Moscow Art Theatre to America in 1923–1924 was instrumental in bringing about significant changes in the way American actors approached their craft. When the company returned to Moscow, a few Moscow Art Theatre actors remained in New York and became influential acting teachers using Stanislavski's techniques. Their students, in turn, became strong advocates of Stanislavski-based training.

By 1931 the Group Theatre was organized in New York along the lines of the Moscow Art Theatre and emulated that theatre's belief in ensemble productions and especially Stanislavski's devotion to emphasizing the inner truth of the character. The Group Theatre was active for ten years, during which time the Stanislavski system became firmly established in America.

After World War II, in 1947, the Actors Studio was founded by three former members of the defunct Group Theatre: Bobby Lewis, Cheryl Crawford, and Elia Kazan. Lee Strasberg, an important member of the Group Theatre, later became the Actors Studio's dominant acting teacher, while Kazan emerged as the most significant stage director of the postwar era. The Actors Studio became the training ground for hundreds of important stage and film actors including Marlon Brando, James Dean, Karl Malden, and Marilyn Monroe. Even actors and directors not immediately connected with the Group Theatre or the Actors Studio were influenced by the dynamic effect of their approach to theatre.

While the Actors Studio continues today it does not have the same theatrical impact it had from 1947 to the late 1960s. The Actors Studio was instrumental in refining the American approach to acting and actor training and remains as the foundation for most actor training today.

▬ PSYCHOLOGICAL REALISM

Throughout the remainder of the twentieth century, many playwrights and directors in the commercial theatre (and in much of the noncommercial theatre) continued to work in the *modern* style, often called *psychological realism*. These modern directors approached their craft with the belief that the playwright's words were of primary concern. Theirs was a language-oriented theatre in which the playwright's intent, insofar as it could be understood by the director, was the one true guide to play production.

Psychological realism includes these precepts:

- The sights and sounds are generally those one sees and hears in everyday life.
- The audience is expected to accept that what is happening on stage is real.
- People are motivated by psychology and act consistently. Characters may not always understand their own motivations, but the audience does understand them—at least by the end of the play.
- The tone of the play is more or less consistent. Even though stories may be presented out of chronological order, the stories have a unified and clear shape, with action generally rising to a climax.
- The story focuses on an individual who is in an important conflict. Through interaction with others, and through making choices and learning more, this individual comes to some new understanding and the conflict is resolved.
- Science and reason permeate the playwright's determination of truth.

Elia Kazan (1909–2003) and Psychological Realism

Kazan was the last surviving member of the generation of artists that connect contemporary theatre with the Group Theatre and the early years of the Actors Studio. He was the most influential American director of the 1940s, '50s, and '60s, staging landmark productions of plays by Thornton Wilder, Tennessee Williams, and Arthur Miller. During this same era he directed significant films, including *On the Waterfront*, *Gentlemen's Agreement*, and *A Streetcar Named Desire*.

Kazan joined the Group Theatre in 1933 as an apprentice actor after dropping out of the Yale Drama School. With the Group Theatre he acted in a dozen or more productions, including a memorable performance in Clifford Odets' *Waiting for Lefty* (1935). He began his directing career shortly thereafter.

During World War II he directed Wilder's *The Skin of Our Teeth* (1942). After the war he was the most sought after American director of plays, guiding Tennessee Williams' A *Streetcar Named Desire* (1949), *Cat on a Hot Tin Roof* (1955), and *Sweet Bird of Youth* (1959).

With his frequent designer Jo Mielziner, Kazan established a production style known as *theatrical realism* in which the physical production retained a line of reality but eliminated nonessentials. The acting emphasized intense psychological truth.

Elia Kazan earned three Tony awards among a host of other accolades during his long career. In 1999 he was awarded an honorary Oscar for lifetime achievement in film.

This style has been so dominant that it has become commonplace for directors to impose psychological realism on productions of playscripts originating prior to the modern era. The most common examples are the plays of Shakespeare: a famous film of Shakespeare's *Hamlet* interpreted the play rather narrowly through the lens of Sigmund Freud's psychological theory of the Oedipus complex.

While *realism* was and is a popular production ideal, it has not been the only theatrical production style. Once realism gained a foothold, there were important movements that challenged the basic tenets of theatrical modernism, often seen as reactions to realism or as alternatives to realism. The following are examples of four distinct approaches to playwriting and production style.

Expressionism

Expressionism presents the world as seen from one individual's distorted viewpoint. This individual is insane or temporarily undergoing an extreme psychological crisis. Expressionism, then, is an exterior expression of interior chaos. Georg Kaiser (*Gas*), Elmer Rice (*The Adding Machine*), and Georg Buchner (*Woyzeck*) are playwrights who wrote in the expressionist style. Expressionism is also a production style that

presents a distorted scenic universe. Garish colors, jagged angles, and oddly propor-
tioned objects are hallmarks of expressionistic stage design. Realistic playwrights
since expressionism's heyday in the 1920s sometimes incorporate expressionistic
elements in otherwise realistic modern stories.

Epic Theatre

Epic theatre, sometimes called Brechtian theatre, subverts the suspension of disbe-
lief of the modernist theatre in an attempt to engage the audience in political discussion and action. Epic theatre is episodic and anti-illusionistic. It mixes direct address
to the audience with dramatic episodes and telescopes time and place. It tries to
engage the audience, draw them into the dramatic situation, and then abruptly jerk
the audience out of their empathetic response so that they might think about the
political consequences of the dramatic action. Brecht often used songs to disengage
the audience from the dramatic action. This technique is called the *alienation effect*.

Bertolt Brecht's *The Good Woman of Setzuan* is a representative example.
Thornton Wilder's *Our Town* uses alienation to communicate nonpolitical themes.
Remember that the Stage Manager, a narrator who directly addresses the audience,
interrupts the action and focuses attention on Wilder's central ideas.

Surrealism

Surrealism creates a subconscious, dream-like world that is often distorted, moody,
and disjointed. It is a technique that tries to communicate an unconscious inner
world governed not by logic but by intuition and unprocessed feeling. In contrast to
expressionism, surrealism is not necessarily the distorted view of one aberrant character; surrealism uses dream effects to expose or heighten the dramatic impact of a
character's interior states. Surrealism is both a playwriting and a production style.
Laurey's dream ballet at the end of the first act of *Oklahoma!*, for example, is a
dance fantasy, clearly introduced by the song "Out of My Dreams." Laurey *dreams*
of what she fears will happen if she marries the handyman, Judd. The ballet is about
emotion, not logic. It is a surreal moment in a realistic musical, to the extent that a
mid-twentieth-century musical can be realistic.

More recently, Tony Kushner's *Angels in America* used surrealism as part of
its postmodernist mix of styles: two characters meet in each other's dreams; a
valium addict visits an arctic ice floe in a dream where she meets a clarinet-playing
galactic "travel agent"; the ghost of a 1930s partisan of communism, Emma Gold-
man, comes to the hospital of the dying anti-communist Roy Cohn to taunt him.
Most enduring is when a dying man lying in bed sees—dreams?—an angel crashing
through his ceiling. The climax of the play occurs in a bizarre vision of heaven
where that man argues with a choir of angels and wins the argument.

Absurdism

Absurdism is virtually a philosophy, as it views life as hopeless. Individuals are alone in a meaningless universe. Language does not lead to communication. Notable absurdist playwrights include Samuel Beckett (*Waiting for Godot*), Eugene Ionesco (*The Bald Soprano*), and Edward Albee (*Who's Afraid of Virginia Woolf?*). In *The Bald Soprano*, for example, two married couples visit and engage in meaningless banter filled with non sequiturs. This chatter suggests that the characters are not listening to one another, much less understand what is being said. And there is no formal end to the play. Ionesco's last stage direction is to begin the play again.

Some modern theatre blended the four styles discussed above and other anti-real styles as episodes within a psychologically real framework, creating hybrid forms and styles. That is, modern playwrights embraced and incorporated some qualities of these anti-real styles into psychological realism. Even though much of Eugene O'Neill's and Tennessee Williams' plays are realistic, O'Neill's play *The Emperor Jones* is expressionistic while Williams' *Camino Real* is epic.

Directors of the modern era, too, devised productions that did not exactly conform to the realistic worldview. They modified the playwright's given circumstances by changing locale, time, and the play's inherent theatrical conventions. Such directors, for example, include Sir Tyrone Guthrie, Peter Brook, Mark Lamos, Daniel Sullivan, and Orson Welles. In 1937, Welles, for example, set *Julius Cesar* in fascist Italy with contemporary costumes in a heavily edited version of Shakespeare's play.

■ POSTMODERNISM

By the 1960s, another reaction to realism appeared, one that has come to be called postmodernism. For many critics and audience members, postmodernism *is* contemporary theatre. Postmodernism has a purposely unorthodox viewpoint, so it is not surprising that postmodernist works have yet to dominate commercial theatre. Perhaps they never will.

Since this movement is still evolving, it can be difficult to define. (Some critics contend that all the nonpsychologically real styles listed earlier are part of postmodernism, too. This position at least calls into question whether postmodernism is *post* anything.) Some undeniable qualities of postmodernism, however, include the following:

- A basic disregard for a traditional sense of unity.
- A belief in differences and shades of meaning rather than black/white opposites.
- An ironic approach to the making of art—questioning whether art has a lasting effect and whether beauty exists.

Sir Tyrone Guthrie and the Thrust Stage (1900–1971)

Tyrone Guthrie became one of the most respected theatre artists of the twentieth century, earning international acclaim for his direction of classic plays by Greek, English, French, and American authors. He was also adept at directing operas.

Working with his favorite designer, Tanya Moisevitsch, he reintroduced and popularized the thrust stage actor-audience relationship in England, Canada, and the United States. Working first at the Royal Shakespeare Company, he designed (with Moisevitsch) a single architectural unit set with a thrust stage for a series of Shakespeare's history plays.

This temporary thrust stage proved so successful in Guthrie's opinion that when he was asked to direct a medieval Scottish play for the Edinburgh Festival, he located a large banqueting hall in an ancient home and had a thrust stage installed. He was then invited to create a Shakespeare festival in Stratford in Canada. He agreed on the condition that the theatre would have a permanent thrust stage that Moisevitsch would design. The Stratford Shakespeare Festival opened in 1953. Ten years later he inaugurated the Tyrone Guthrie Theatre in Minneapolis with a permanent thrust stage modeled after the one in Canada.

His productions of Shakespeare were characterized almost always by a resetting of the play in another time and place. His modern dress production of *Timon of Athens* in Canada and *Hamlet* in Minnesota were hailed as brilliant.

- A rejection of the ideas of objectivity, reason, certainty, and personal identity.
- A belief that history is not a story of progress but is a story of the struggles of different privileged groups for domination.
- A deep interest in the meaning inherent in signs and in accepted conventions and traditional stories.
- A belief that individual psychology is less important to how characters behave than are social strictures and the structure of language at the time.

As a result of these basic tenets, postmodern theatre is often nonlinear, nonliterary, nonrealistic, nontraditional, and inconclusive; that is, it embraces qualities that are the antithesis of modernism.

Notable postmodern playwrights include Caryl Churchill (*Cloud Nine*, *Top Girls*), Tony Kushner (*Angels in America*), Peter Nichols (*A Day in the Death of Joe Egg*), and Paula Vogel (*Baltimore Waltz, How I Learned to Drive*).

Just as modern directors often staged scripts from earlier eras through the lens of psychological realism, so postmodern directors often restage earlier works— including modern texts—in radical ways. These postmodern directors may maintain that the author's text is just one of many contributions to a production; actors, designers, and the director add as much (or, probably, more) to a theatrical production as do the playwright's linguistic inventions. The playscript, these contemporary directors contend, can only add words to the theatrical event, while other artists will inflect the words, add facial expressions, gestures, other nonlinguistic sounds, clothing, light, color, movement, pace, tempo, and the telling arrangement of people in and through space. Surely these contributions exceed, or at least equal, in importance the playwright's words. In fact, many postmodern directors cut, rearrange, and/or alter the playscript. Some postmodern directors present the playwright's words intact but surround the playscript with a startling new environment, context, and style so that the playwright's world may be unrecognizable. One postmodern director, for example, staged a good deal of Tennessee Williams' *A Streetcar Named Desire* in a bathtub complete with water.

Perhaps inevitably, the gestures of postmodernism are stealing into otherwise modern plays and productions, resulting in hybrid forms. This assimilation adds to the difficulty of saying clearly what postmodernism is and what theatre is postmodern.

■ CONTEMPORARY DIRECTORS

The careers of directors today reflect the wide variety of playscripts available for production, the multiplicity of production styles, and the striking assortment of theatre spaces and producing organizations. Audience members, too, don't have to pledge allegiance to one approach or style of theater. For example, theatre venues range from 99-seat found spaces to 3,000-seat touring houses with gilt prosceniums. Prosperous theatrical organizations can be amateur, academic, nonprofit, or commercial. Producing groups vary from seat-of-the-pants to established. Many directors move readily among these venues: small, not-for-profit professional theatres; institutional, even venerable, regional centers; Broadway, Off Broadway, and the road. They direct plays from classical Greece as well as those that were written only yesterday.

Once directing was a man's domain—a white man who was heterosexual (or at least hid behind a mask of heterosexuality). Theatre a half-century ago was little different from any other part of American culture. Theatre may not have easily welcomed minorities, gay people, and women, but talented artists have through the brilliance of their talent, skills, and social activism elbowed their way into the mainstream.

Successful performing and directing styles have seldom before shown as much variety as they do today. Psychological realism is alive and well. Musical comedies and revues thrive. Politically engaged theatre continues to try to change public discourse. Classic plays are reinterpreted for our times and tastes, often in ways that shock audiences as much as any new script might. And new scripts offer postmodern, still-evolving ideas of contemporary life. The following examination of three artistically successful contemporary directors indicates the range and diversity of the directing profession in the first decade of the twenty-first century.

JoAnne Akalaitis: The Process Is All

JoAnne Akalaitis, one of the best-known postmodern directors in America, devoted 20 years to working with the like-minded colleagues of Mabou Mines, of which she is a cofounder and was a co-artistic director. The group describes itself as "an avant-garde theatre company emphasizing the creation of new theatre pieces from original texts and the theatrical use of existing texts staged from a specific point of view." For Mabou Mines Akalaitis created and directed *Dead End Kids* and nearly a dozen other theatre pieces.

JoAnne Akalaitis has worked in important regional theatres across America and in Europe. For a short time she was artistic director of the New York Public Theatre. In one of her most noted productions, Samuel Beckett's *Endgame* for the American Repertory Theatre in Boston, she altered the setting described in the playwright's text. Instead of "an empty room with two small windows," Akalaitis set the play in a cluttered subway station with an overture and incidental music by Phillip Glass. Beckett learned of these changes and tried to have the courts stop the production. A compromise was reached in which the author's objection was printed in the program.

As a director, she is most interested in the rehearsal process. Akalaitis often begins a production with exercises for the actors that move them beyond a concern for the surface values of a playscript. These improvisations lead her instinctive creative vision. Her productions are often surreal and nonlinear, even when she is directing Shakespeare.

Julie Taymor: East Meets West

Best known for her direction of *The Lion King* (1998), Julie Taymor is also a world-recognized designer of costumes, masks, and puppets. For her work in *The Lion King,* Taymor won a Tony award for best costume design and was the first female to win a Tony award for direction of a musical.

In the first musical number, "Circle of Life," the Lion King summons the animals, all of whom are actor-puppets. The giraffes are actors walking on stilts—they appear to be ten feet tall. A huge elephant lumbers down a theatre aisle propelled by four actors, one in each foot. The magical result is a production that avoids the literal translation from an animated film to a nonliteral, imaginative stage production. Disney's *The Lion King* has been produced all over the world.

After studying mime in Paris and acting in New York, Taymor received a fellowship to study theatre and puppetry in eastern Europe and Asia, particularly Indonesia. When she returned to America she launched her career as a director/designer.

Her productions are characterized by a mixture of actors, masks, puppets, and magnificent stage images. Julie Taymor believes that there is meaning in the medium of theatre itself as well as in the process of creating a production with actors. She often creates characters first through sculpting and drawing and then introduces the actor to her images.

On Broadway she directed *The Green Bird* (an adaptation of Carlo Gozzi's adaption of a commedia dell'arte script) and *Juan Darien: A Carnival Mask* (based on a Latin American folk tale), for which she received Tony nominations for direction and scene design. Shakespeare appears frequently in her list of credits, including *The Tragedy of Titus Andronicus* on stage and on film. The film version, called *Titus*, starred Anthony Hopkins and Jessica Lange. She also directed the acclaimed film *Freda*.

George C. Wolfe: Playwright and Director

When George Wolfe became artistic director of the Public Theatre in New York, he returned to the theatre that produced his best-known playscript, *The Colored Museum*, a collection of revue sketches on the African-American experience. On Broadway he directed and wrote *Jelly's Last Jam* (Tony nominations in both categories), and directed a revival of *On the Town* and both parts of Tony Kushner's *Angels in America* (Tony award for direction). Wolfe used the Public Theatre to

George C. Wolfe and Diversity

This prolific director has made his position clear about a theatre devoted to the production of plays by dead white men and administered by white heterosexual men. Wolfe is black and an acknowledged gay man. What follows is an excerpt from a speech Wolfe made to a national meeting of black theatre artists.

I hate the word diversity. The need to come up with a term to express the inclusion of people is based on the absurd fact that in America, European culture is held up as the only true legitimate culture. Consequently, when cultural institutions decide to invite people of color or what I like to call the "others" to the party, a word needs to be crafted and that word has become diversity.

Point of fact, the whole scenario should be reversed. Cultural institutions should be forced to explain why they are excluding people. I would love to hear theatres explain why, in their whole histories, they haven't presented stories of people of color from this country—and not "Negroes" from somewhere else. I'd really like to hear why. How do you rationalize that in a city like New York? Because if you are not telling my story, not telling the stories of all the different people in this country, then you can't call yourself an American theatre. You are an elitist white institution and should hang a banner outside calling yourself that.

I think, by and large, people in the theatre are liberal. But liberal intentions or not, they don't want to share the power. There has been a long history of white artists extolling the cultures of non-whites. But, ultimately, when you strip it down, it's cultural colonization. Until people from those cultures are involved in making decisions as directors, writers, producers, artistic directors—and there are very few of them—there will be no substantial change.

bring the work of minority artists to greater recognition: more African-American, Latin, Asian, gay and lesbian, and feminist playwrights and directors enlivened the New York theatrical scene because of Wolfe's programming.

George Wolfe's biggest commercial success so far is *Bring in 'da Noise/Bring in 'da Funk*, which he conceived and directed at the Public Theatre. The production then moved to Broadway, where it ran for over a year and won four Tony awards, including one for direction. *Noise/Funk* is structured as a revue of the history of African-Americans in America. Projections of text, original music, poetry and songs, street drummers, and exciting tap dancing energized this postmodern production.

His training in New York University's musical theatre program most likely influenced his penchant for musicals, episodic drama, and the revue structure. His staging of *Elaine Stritch: At Liberty*, a one-person show with music, won a special Tony award. He also directed Suzan-Lori Parks' episodically structured *Top Dog/Underdog*, which won the Pulitzer Prize for drama. His productions, including *Angels in America*, are characterized by surreal juxtapositions and a nonlinear structure. Certainly the physical productions are not solely realistic.

These three directors are only a sample of the variety of talent and directing viewpoints that are central to theatre in the twenty-first century.

A RECOMMENDATION

For the purposes of the first directing experiences, beginning directors should initiate their work in the dominant style of our times, psychological realism. The dominance of psychological realism in film and television means that even students new to the theatre have a wealth of experience in this production style as audience members. Within this strategy we have the support of many leading figures of postmodern theatre, who contend that psychological realism should be mastered first. At the very least, novice directors will begin to understand realism and the idea that other theatrical styles are reactions or alternatives to realism.

INDEX